Spitfire Groundcrew
Under Fire

Spitfire Groundcrew Under Fire

An RAF 'Erk's' War from the Battle of Britain to D-Day and Operation Bodenplatte

Joe Roddis with Mark Hillier

AIR WORLD

First published in Great Britain in 2024 by
Pen & Sword Air World
An imprint of Pen & Sword Books Limited
Yorkshire – Philadelphia

ISBN 978 1 39905 986 2

A CIP catalogue record for this book is
available from the British Library

Typeset by Mac Style
Printed in the UK by CPI Group (UK) Ltd, Croydon, CR0 4YY.

Pen & Sword Books Limited incorporates the imprints of After the Battle,
Atlas, Archaeology, Aviation, Discovery, Family History, Fiction, History,
Maritime, Military, Military Classics, Politics, Select, Transport, True Crime,
Air World, Frontline Publishing, Leo Cooper, Remember When, Seaforth
Publishing, The Praetorian Press, Wharncliffe Local History, Wharncliffe
Transport, Wharncliffe True Crime and White Owl.

For a complete list of Pen & Sword titles please contact

PEN & SWORD BOOKS LIMITED
47 Church Street, Barnsley, South Yorkshire, S70 2AS, England
E-mail: enquiries@pen-and-sword.co.uk
Website: www.pen-and-sword.co.uk
or
PEN AND SWORD BOOKS
1950 Lawrence Road, Havertown, PA 19083, USA
E-mail: uspen-and-sword@casematepublishers.com
Website: www.penandswordbooks.com

In memory of Joseph Roddis
30 May 1921–19 April 2017

Contents

Foreword

The ground crew who joined 485 (NZ) Squadron in March 1941 either volunteered or were conscripted into the role of servicing aircraft – a far cry from the civilian life they were accustomed.

Unlike the Spitfire pilots in the squadron, who were in the main New Zealanders, this was not the case for the ground crew. Many of the ground crew personnel, including men such as Joe Roddis, were with the squadron for the duration until it was disbanded in 1945.

As pilots, we were so very dependent on the ground crew and close associations were formed. The ground crew boys regularly serviced aircraft through the night to ensure that they were operational.

Squadrons usually had eighteen aircraft. A standard fifty-hour service took about twenty-four hours. In addition, damaged planes required a higher level of service and new planes underwent a complete commissioning process. The backlog of work was consequently high. The dedication and effort put in by the ground crew was not appreciated by the population at large.

The New Zealand pilots by their nature enjoyed the company of the ground crew. There was a rapport quite unlike that of other squadrons. They were treated as equals by commanding officer and pilots alike. On occasions when misdemeanours were committed (contrary to regulation and brought to account by the hierarchy!) we, as pilots, would ensure there were no grounds to pursue.

An early photograph of Sergeant Doug Brown, later to become squadron leader, who served with Nos. 130 and 485 (NZ) squadrons. Doug served with Joe on 485 (NZ) Squadron and, as with all the pilots, he held Joe and the groundcrew in high regard. Doug Completed two tours and carried out over 280 operational sorties, with some 650 hours on Spitfires. He was also Mentioned in Despatches for his distinguished service. (*Hamish Brown*)

As pilots, while we flew the Spitfires, without the dedication and enthusiastic support of ground crew our operational flying would have been badly impaired due to lack of confidence in the reliability of our aircraft whether it be engine, oxygen, radio or armament.

They were the forgotten heroes!

Flight Lieutenant Doug Brown RNZAF

The Flight Tech

The Lords of the air they call us,
They speak of our growing fame,
The front page of every paper,
Is adorned with some pilot's name.
Connected with some deed of valour
Performed high up in the sky.
The usual are Heinkels and Dorniers
Crashing to earth to die.
Here's one chap who gets no medal
You never hear his name.
He does not fly in the pale blue sky
Or pose for the news in a plane.
His job cannot be called romantic
So he's not in the public eye.
But your heroes can't do without him
And I tell you the reason why ....
He inspects the kit every morning,
He fills the tank each night,
He keeps the engine running sweet,
He keeps the pressure right.
He's up at the break of dawn,
He's still there when twilight fades
Pulling his weight to keep the crate
Ready to fly on its raids.

So next time you see a picture
Of plane and its smiling crew
Remember the bloke who keeps it afloat
Although he's an AC2

Next time you praise a pilot
As the enemy falls a wreck
Remember the guy you did not see ....
Yours Truly – a humble Flight Tech.

Anon

Acknowledgements

This book has been illustrated with images kindly supplied by Hamish Brown, Max Collett of 485 (NZ) Squadron, Edward McManus, who set up the wonderful website www.BBM.org.uk, and Peter R. Arnold. I would like to thank Martin Mace and John Grehan for help and support, Chris Goss for information and images on the Middle Wallop attack, and Dilip Sarkar MBE FRHistS FRAeS for permission to use the quotes from Fred Roberts. Finally, as always, thanks must go to my lovely family who allow me time to produce books.

Introduction

This book is a tribute to an exceptional man and is dedicated to his memory. Joe Roddis was one of a kind – they broke the mould when he was created. He was an individual who told it as it was and not one to embellish a story. But he did not need to, as he had seen and experienced the dangers of war at the sharp end. Not fighting in the trenches, but as an RAF ground crew member.

Some might not appreciate that these stalwarts were there in all weathers servicing and fixing front line aircraft, or that they were at times under fire from the enemy. Joe was no exception. From 1944 onwards Joe and his comrades often had to overcome hardship, living in cold damp tents, never being able to dry out clothing, suffering from colds and viruses as well as unsanitary conditions. The food was not too great either, but these men knew that without their support, determination and fortitude, ingenuity and loyalty, the air war would grind to a halt.

Joe and I met in 2008, just after the completion of my first book. He was proudly wearing his squadron blazer, with its 485 (NZ) Squadron badge, and his well-deserved medals on his chest. I quickly established that his career started in 1939, that he served during the Battle of Britain in a front line fighter squadron, before going on to work with Spitfires for the rest of the war. He headed out to the Continent after D-Day with 485 (NZ) Squadron, this being a period in which he faced constant danger. Post-war, Joe served on Vampires, then as a crew chief on the RAF's Boeing B-29 Washingtons, before heading out to Malaya with 617 Squadron, which was equipped with the English Electric Canberra, and finishing his career on the Vickers Valiant. His favourite aircraft, though, remained his beloved Spitfire.

Though Joe had an exceptionally interesting time in the RAF, he was not inclined to shout about it. Likewise, one constant in our friendship over the years was the ability to be honest and frank with each other; as mentioned above, Joe certainly told it as it was. He had a very endearing character and we had a special bond. He became part of my family, along with his partner Betty who sadly pre-deceased Joe.

I first helped Joe with his story in 2012; people could not believe how lucky Joe had been, many were totally engaged by his story and the honesty in which he portrayed his experiences. Joe always said he enjoyed his war and loved to talk to people about his involvement. He was humble to the last and never asked for any special attention or to be singled out, a feature of so many of his generation.

I hope that in our re-telling of his story Joe will be seen as a 17-year-old lad, fresh-faced and recently enlisted in the RAF, who went on to face death many times during his war. This book focuses on some of those pivotal life and death moments in his career.

Over the years of knowing Joe I have listened to many of his stories and had lots of chance luckily to get down on paper his thoughts and memories. Since first exploring Joe's wartime career, I have had the chance to gather and collate far more information and expanded on his story.

Joe had a deep respect for the pilots on his squadron and would never have wanted anyone to think that his story was out there to trump their efforts – far from it. That said, most of the veteran 485 (NZ) Squadron pilots I have spoken to or interviewed over the years had nothing but the utmost respect for their groundcrew. The pilots were also keen to point out their appreciation for the hard work, tenacity, and bravery shown by these chaps who were also at risk from enemy action. The aim of this book, therefore, is to highlight the role of these wonderful stalwarts of the wartime RAF squadrons, men who were often overlooked but were an essential cog in the wheel.

One could cite many examples of groundcrew sacrifice during the Second World War, but one that is, quite literally, closest to home for me were the losses at RAF Tangmere during the Luftwaffe attack on 16 August 1940. Many times, I have wandered through the graveyard at St. Andrews Church at Tangmere and gazed upon the final resting place of the airmen killed on this day. That day, the pre-war RAF fighter station was bombed by a large force of Junkers Ju 87s which inflicted severe damage on the airfield. All the hangars were completely destroyed or badly damaged. During the course of the action, the station workshops, sick quarters, water pumping station and Officers' Mess were wrecked, and the power, water and sanitation systems were put out of action. Remarkably, despite the damage the airfield remained operational. Tragically, ten servicemen and three civilians were killed, and another twenty injured. All of the servicemen killed were groundcrew.

Joe joined the Royal Air Force in February 1939 during a time of great change. Squadrons within the RAF re-equipping with more modern fighters, the old trusty biplanes being replaced with all metal monoplanes such as the Spitfire. Churchill had warned of what was about to come and the RAF was building up its strength in preparation for possible war.

The Luftwaffe had gained considerable experience in combat during the Spanish Civil War and as Adolf Hitler moved on Poland the might of air power was enshrined in the history books. It became clear that whoever had command of the air had the upper hand on the battlefield. German aircraft appeared to be more advanced and superior in numbers to those in the RAF, but the Luftwaffe had not counted on the tenacity and dogged determination of the British, Commonwealth and Allied pilots.

In 1939, RAF squadrons were committed to help defend France along with regiments of the British Army as part of the British Expeditionary Force. Their aim was to help stem a possible German thrust into France and Belgium. It was obvious from early operations that some of the combat aircraft operated by the squadrons in the RAF were too slow and under armed, but valuable experience of aerial combat techniques gained at this point in time would stand the RAF pilots in good stead for the forthcoming Luftwaffe onslaught in the summer of 1940.

Pilots had to be combat ready, ground crews trained and efficient. Keeping an operational squadron ready for action was certainly a team effort. Behind every pilot would have been fitters, riggers, armourers, drivers, cooks, and storemen, amongst other trades, all of whom had to pull together as a team. The ultimate goal was to keep their aircraft at the dispersal, serviceable and with a pilot ready to be scrambled at a moment's notice. The groundcrew shared in their squadron's successes and losses, but did not look for, or often were not given any recognition for their role. That had, however, the satisfaction of knowing that they had done their bit.

Joe nearly came a cropper several times during the Battle of Britain, but when he retold the stories, he was honest about his feelings and that he was often scared, though he also thought of it as an adventure. He often would pause and reflect on each story and you could see that he was contemplating his experiences and luck at getting through the war relatively unscathed.

Even in his 90s he was a regular attender at the Boultbee Flight Academy where he would discuss his experiences with the engineers on the Spitfire, the engines he had worked on and even started up a Mk.IX in front of an admiring crowd.

Over the years, Joe appeared on TV, including in programmes about the Battle of Britain with David Jason and *The Spitfire* with John Sergeant. It was Joe's involvement with *Spitfire Ace* and RDF media that re-sparked a friendship with Betty sixty years after they parted company at Worthing railway station during the war. Betty Wood had been Joe's wartime dancing partner and she too was also a serving WAAF.

The Grace Spitfire, ML407, featured in this programme and it was Carolyn Grace who ensured that Joe was involved in the filming as he had an association with this aircraft at Selsey in 1944. Betty was at home watching the TV and spotted Joe, having not seen him since 1944 when they went their own separate ways. As so many years had passed she initially didn't recognise him, but remembered the name. Having lost her husband and now living alone, she re-contacted Joe and they met some time after, this time at Chichester railway station. They rekindled their friendship and moved in together.

It was a privilege to have had the opportunity to get to know Joe. Sadly, he passed away at his home, at the age of 95, on 19 April 2017. His last ten years had been a roller-coaster of flying, interviews, guest appearances, signings and talks about his RAF career. If you were one of those lucky enough to have met him or had chance to make his acquaintance you will know what a special man he was.

This book is put together from interviews I conducted with Joe, some of his own diary entries and correspondence, and photographs from his own collection, of which I am now proudly the custodian. It gives a unique insight into the life of "just an ordinary erk" as Joe often referred to himself. However, you will discover that his experience was far from ordinary, and that groundcrew often faced operational dangers and job-related risk. I have no doubt that there are many other stories untold, of groundcrew and their contribution to the war effort, without whom the aircraft that gave us air superiority would not have flown.

The words that sum up Joe and his contribution to the Battle of Britain are contained within a copy of Wing Commander Bob Doe DSO, DFC & Bar's autobiography *Fighter*

Pilot, Bob had served with Joe on 234 Squadron during the Battle of Britain. Inside this copy, Bob once wrote: "To Joe, without whom we would not have won the Battle of Britain". This is undoubtedly a fitting tribute to not only Joe, but also his groundcrew colleagues who played their part in the Allies' victory in the Second World War. They are, it could be said, the forgotten heroes.

Mark Hillier,
Fontwell, 2024.

Chapter 1

In the Beginning

I joined the Royal Air Force at the age of 17, signing on at West Drayton on 20 February 1939. I then went on to do my Basic Training – square bashing – at RAF Driffield in Yorkshire, my home county. There we were issued with the rest of our uniforms, a full set of webbing, a .303 Lee Enfield rifle, a large bayonet for drill purposes, or except when on guard duty, and instructed about how to clean your kit. On top of this, we were taught about all the 101 other things that would eventually make you into a good airman. After three months we 'passed out' from the course and were posted.

I did my trade training with quite a few other chaps at RAF St Athan in Wales. There we were taught about everything to do with the engines on the aircraft currently in service in the RAF.

It was whilst I was at St Athan that war was declared on 3 September 1939. My course was shortened and I was posted to RAF Leconfield where I joined 234 Squadron.

Joe at the age of 17, just after enlisting in the RAF. This photograph was taken at RAF Driffield.

At that time the squadron had a few odd types of aircraft, including Avro Tutors, Miles Magisters, Fairey Battles, Gloster Gauntlets amongst other biplanes that I can't remember the names of. We occupied one of the five huge hangars off of the perimeter track from which we operated the aircraft.

No.234 Squadron was originally formed at RNAS Tresco in the Scilly Isles on 20 August 1918. At the time the main role for the squadron was patrolling the Western Approaches, a task it returned to in early 1940. It was disbanded again in 1919. Its re-birth began at RAF Leconfield on 30 October 1939. Though initially equipped with a variety of aircraft, in due course the squadron was re-equipped with Spitfires, much to the excitement of both pilots and groundcrew alike. These were given the squadron identity codes 'AZ' on the fuselage.

When the weather was suitable, we seemed to do a lot of flying. When the weather or something else prevented this, then we would sit in a huge crew room in the hangar. There we would read, chat or play cards until it was time to go to Smokey-Joe's little cafe on the airfield as it was preferable to the NAAFI.

Our living and sleeping accommodation was generally five to a room. We were then housed in what had been the RAF married quarters, the previous occupants and their families having been moved out for the duration when war started.

I was by then 18 years of age, a fully trained flight mechanic, raring to go. The only excitement we got was when they ceremoniously wheeled our most up to date aircraft – a Fairey Battle – out of the hangar. It was taxied round the perimeter track, and some equally frustrated young pilot and crew was sent aloft in it to get some experience on a 'modern' monoplane! I was put with an experienced corporal to be taught what my job would be as an engine mechanic.

We were envious of the squadron that occupied the next but one hangar from ours. It was 616 (South Yorkshire) Squadron, whose aircraft at that time carried the codes letters 'QJ'. They were fully operational with their Spitfire Mk.Is, and to see them 'Scramble' a section of three aircraft was magic.

An Auxiliary Air Force unit, 616 (South Yorkshire) Squadron had moved to RAF Leconfield on 21 October 1939. It received its first Spitfire on 8 November, with ten more arriving from 66 Squadron on the 14th of the month, allowing the pilots to complete the preparations for operational flying.

They were a squadron of practically fully-trained weekend pilots and the Auxiliary squadrons were obviously high up in the queue for Spitfires and Hurricanes. Unfortunately, they were responsible for 234 Squadron's first fatal accident.

It was a lovely day weather-wise, and we were out flying our selection of biplanes from our grassed area in front of the hangar when 616 fired a red Verey light, which was the signal to scramble. I witnessed every moment of what followed from where I was working on an aircraft.

The section of 616 Squadron at readiness was arranged on the grass in front of their hangar, facing into wind, when the red light went up. No runway was used by the scrambling pilots – it was just a case of start-up and take-off. The right-hand aircraft passed in front of us to the left, about fifty yards away, and was just about ready to lift off.

As I said earlier, normally it was magic to watch. But then I suddenly noticed that our yellow Miles Magister was taxiing out on to the airfield from our hangar. The Spitfire was just about airborne when it hit the 'Maggy' where the port wing joins the fuselage and cockpit area.

The 'Maggy' disintegrated in a shower of plywood and fabric. It was literally flattened. The Spitfire tipped on its nose, shattering its prop, before running on for a good few yards before stopping. The Spitfire's pilot climbed out and ran towards the Magister – that's when we all started running too.

Lord knows how many revs the prop had been running at as it sliced through the cockpit of the 'Maggy'. Sadly there was not much left of the pilot. He was a young Canadian officer called Coysh – very tragic!

The son of Reginald R. Coysh and Ida Coysh, Pilot Officer David Whittier Coysh was 22-years-old at the time of his death on 21 February 1940. His grave can be found in Torquay Cemetery. The other crewman in the Magister, Flying Officer J.S. Bell, survived, though injured. The Magister had the serial number N3849, while the Spitfire was K9988.

At this stage we were, with our mixture of aircraft, still a non-operational squadron. As a result we were therefore working normal hours of 8 a.m. to 5 p.m.., Monday to Friday, and spending our free time between our billet and the canteen or NAAFI.

Our forages away from the airfield were usually spent walking to the nearest town, which was Beverley, about two or three miles away. There we would quaff a few pints of falling down liquid! I was paid 2/- per day, of which I sent 1/- to my mother which she deposited in the Post Office Savings Bank for me. Hence my total weekly cash spent was 7/-, which went on soap, toothpaste, shoe polish, metal polish, stamps and writing paper. Also, envelopes, ink and the occasional tea and wad or cake in the NAAFI or at Smokey Joe's.

Occasionally I would receive a Postal Order from my parents, grand-parents, or uncles and aunts, these ranging in value from 6d to 2/6 (half a crown). These meant that I was rich then, causing me to sally forth with my two roommates, 'Nosey Parker' and 'Lofty', both Halton apprentices, and walk to the Green Dragon public house.

It was very popular with the groundcrew and we'd play darts, Shove ha'penny, or skittles and drink about two pints of mild beer. There were quite a few pubs in Beverley, all situated around the town square. The other popular one, mainly visited by the aircrew and Senior Non-Commissioned Officers (SNCOs), was the Commercial Hotel. Pubs then closed at 10 p.m. and we'd sing our way back to camp, quietening down as we neared the Guard Room – and remaining thus until we were safely in our beds!

The food in the Airmen's Mess at Leconfield was excellent and being out on the airfield all day we ate everything and practically anything that was served up. Sometimes when I was really 'well off' I'd go with a couple of mates to Hull by bus and see a film or look around the shops. When I got leave, I'd get the train from Hull to my home in Sheffield for seven days, but would soon be looking forward to getting back to camp and my mates.

By the end of 1939 the squadron started to get short-nosed Bristol Blenheims. After a training period for both air and ground crews, we started to do shipping protection sorties. The air gunners at that time were mainly AC1s (Aircraftman 1st Class) and LACs (Leading Aircraftmen) who wore a brass winged bullet on their jacket sleeve. For this they received the princely sum of 6d per day!

Gradually the motley assortment of biplanes seemed to just disappear from the squadron, and we got on with servicing and flying the Blenheims. At that point in time it was my job to look after the Blenheims' radial engines and I loved the work. That was until one evening, when, on returning from a night out at the Green Dragon, we were told to go straight to the hangar. We were not to stop off on the way to change out of our best blue uniform as something very urgent and important was afoot!

The hangar was a hive of activity, ablaze with light. The Blenheims that were packed in there were being worked on by all trades and being made ready for despatch to Finland to help the Finns in their struggle against Russia. We even painted out the RAF roundels and replaced them with the Finnish markings of pale blue swastikas. We learnt later that the Russians overran the Finns about a month after we sent our Blenheims.

This was the time of the Winter War between the Russians and the Finns. It ended in March 1940 with the signing of the Moscow Peace Treaty. As part of this agreement, Finland handed over 11% of its pre-war territory and 30% of its economic assets. Russian losses were high. Interestingly, the Finns went on to build the Blenheim under licence, some fifty-five in total, as receiving the British-built examples.

In March 1940 we began to receive our replacement aircraft and when we saw the Spitfires arriving, we couldn't have been prouder or happier. Eighteen brand-new Spitfires Mk.Is! Everybody was over the moon. We crawled all over them, taking the cowlings off and drooling over the Merlins. We couldn't get enough of them.

The arrival of the Spitfires also meant that a lot of hard work followed for everyone. Familiarization for both air and ground crew kept us in the hangar for some time. But the day soon came when we were ready to start flying. The squadron code letters 'AZ' had been painted on all of the aircraft, as well as the individual identity letters A to M for 'A' Flight and N to Z for 'B' Flight.

The aircraft were flown continually for pilots to gain operational experience, though this of course depended on the weather. Groundcrew practised carrying out first and second line servicing to become proficient in all aspects of keeping an operational Spitfire airborne – after all, a fighter aircraft was of no use just sitting on the airfield.

Sometime towards the middle of April 1940 we were to move to RAF Church Fenton, which was still in Yorkshire, to convince command that we were fully prepared and competent enough to become fully operational. During our short stay at Church Fenton, when a day's flying finished, the Spits were flown to a large empty field a few miles away. This was for dispersal away from the main airfield in case of enemy raids.

The field was in a small village called Sherburn-in-Elmet, which is to the south-west of Church Fenton. The pilots would fly there, park their aircraft, and then return to Church Fenton by RAF transport. We, the groundcrew, would be taken

Joe reunited with a Blenheim 1F at Duxford shortly after receiving the *Légion d'Honneur* for his part in the D-Day operations. No.234 Squadron had Blenheim 1Fs from October 1939 through to May 1940. (*Mark Hillier Collection*)

there to service, top up with fuel and oil, and do the after flight inspections. We would stay the night with the aircraft, and by the time the pilots arrived next morning we would have the Spits ready to go back to Church Fenton.

Hurricanes and Lysanders flew in quite frequently from squadrons that had been operational supporting the British Expeditionary Force in France. Their pilots had some pretty awful stories to tell.

Finally, on 8 May 1940 we learned that the squadron was now to become operational, albeit daytime only to start with. This change in status also brought about a move south to RAF St Eval in Cornwall. We groundcrew made the journey by rail, travelling via London. At St Eval, the Spits were kept at dispersal and commenced some serious flying. The armourers were now doing their work for real and no longer for practice!

The squadron was now tasked with carrying out patrols over the Western Approaches, this being an area of the Atlantic Ocean lying immediately to the west of Ireland and parts of Great Britain, and up through the English Channel to protect the convoys bringing essential supplies. The squadron undertook these patrols from first light right through to the hours of darkness. It was at St Eval that Joe encountered his first Luftwaffe raid.

Aircraftman Joe Roddis at St Eval after his arrival from Leconfield. He is standing outside the barrack blocks, which were very basic and heated with a stove in the centre of the building. Joe recalled everyone pulling in the beds towards the stoves to keep their feet warm at night. (*Mark Hillier Collection*)

Chapter 2

The First of Nine Lives, St Eval and Nazi Bombs

Life No.9

Joe often reflected on his initial view that RAF St Eval was a sleepy backwater and that the squadron had been posted fairly out of the way. He often said that he had never expected to see any enemy action while stationed there.

In fact, it was not long before he was to witness at close quarters the effect of enemy bombing, a first blooding if you like. Although Joe recalled that the aircraft involved were Dornier Do 17s, they were in fact mostly Junkers Ju 88s. The Luftwaffe raid on St Eval recalled by Joe occurred on 12 July 1940, when a single Ju 88 dropped eight bombs. It was the first occasion that the airfield was bombed. One account states that the County Controller was at St. Eval and his car was covered with mud from the crater. The intruder was subsequently attacked by two Spitfires and beat a hasty retreat.

Subsequent attacks on St Eval occurred on 21 August 1940, after 234 Squadron and Joe had moved on to RAF Middle Wallop. The raiders returned the following day, the airfield being hit by fourteen high explosive bombs and 200 incendiaries, marking one of the worst raids St Eval was to endure during the war.

But for Joe, his account returns to the events of 12 July 1940.

We were billeted in a row of long wooden huts, about seven or eight of them, on the airfield. These were bombed early one morning without any warning! We were awakened by the sound of low flying aircraft and the crunch of bombs getting nearer each time. We dashed outside, it was about 6 a.m., and saw incendiaries dropping all around us. Some landed on the hut roofs and others on the ground. We kicked them of the huts and out of harm's way.

We heard another aircraft approaching. We were not far away from the hangars and we saw a Dornier 17 [*sic*] fly very low past the opening, but he didn't seem to drop any bombs.

The stick of bombs that got us all out of bed didn't injure any of our chaps. The last bomb scored a direct hit on the end hut which was occupied by the NAAFI girls.

The raid was over as quickly as it had started and a siren soon sounded the 'all clear'. They would have done a lot more damage had they attacked our dispersed Spitfires, but fortunately they didn't.

We had other sporadic raids by one or two bombers. The clothing store was hit and a few other buildings on the main camp suffered various degrees of damage, but they were just nuisance raids really.

The best way to get around an RAF station was by bike. Here Joe poses with his bike at RAF St Athan in 1940. (*Mark Hillier Collection*)

The squadron also had its first success in July, when, I seem to remember, Ken Dewhurst managed to intercept a Ju 88, but I don't think he shot it down, though he gave it some scratch marks.

Soon after this Pat Hughes, Keith Lawrence and another sergeant pilot whose name I can't remember [Sergeant Bailey from the ORB] shared our first proper 'kill' of the war. I remember Lawrence chasing another out to sea a few days later and making a claim. We were as proud as punch that we were part of the RAF's success and doing something. However, we didn't always get it right!

There were other aircraft at St Eval with us, including some Swordfish torpedo carriers and Bristol Beauforts of 217 Squadron. They closely resembled a Ju 88 in the air and once a Ju 88 did get into the circuit with them. Three of our Spitfires were scrambled, and I bet some of the crews didn't forget that day in a hurry.

A hasty snapshot of a low-flying Heinkel He 111 taken during the Battle of Britain. Joe was to be chased across the airfield by a stick of bombs dropped by a raider such as this whilst at RAF Middle Wallop – he was driving a fuel bowser at the time! (*Mark Hillier Collection*)

A photograph of Pilot Officer Keith Lawrence, sent to Joe Roddis by Bob Doe. Keith was a New Zealander and Joe would often chat with him. With his training completed, Lawrence joined 234 Squadron at Leconfield. Lawrence shared in the destruction of a Ju 88 on 8 July, the squadron's first victory. On 12 July he damaged a Ju 88, followed by a Me 110 damaged on 24 August, and then a Me 109 destroyed and a Do 17 damaged 7 September. Shortly after this, Lawrence was posted to 603 Squadron at Hornchurch. On 15 September, his first sortie with 603, he claimed a Me 109 destroyed and two others damaged. Lawrence was posted to 421 Flight, then forming at Hawkinge, on 8 October 1940. On 23 November he damaged a Me 110. The tables were turned during a weather reconnaissance over Ramsgate on 26 November, when he was shot down by Me 109s. The Spitfire disintegrated and Lawrence found himself falling. He manged to deploy his parachute open, and, landing in the sea, burst open a dye sachet, colouring the water. He was picked up by a minesweeper and taken to Ramsgate, where he was admitted to hospital with his right arm dislocated and his right leg broken. Lawrence was later to serve on Malta and was awarded a DFC. (*Mark Hillier Collection*)

To make a positive identification we watched our aircraft fly up to a Beaufort, circle around it, confirm it was 'one of ours' and then head on to the next one. This happened for about ten to fifteen minutes, but we never did see what happened to the Ju 88. He must have slipped off as secretly as he slipped in.

From our dispersal we could look across to the naval airfield at St Merryn, which, also known as HMS *Vulture*, was at this stage of the war being used by the Fleet Air Arm to train aircraft carrier fighter and bomber crews. One day we had a grandstand view of a raid in progress there. The German aircraft just flew in, one after the other, dropped their bombs and then departed leaving a lot of smoking Fleet Air Arm aircraft behind them.

It was on this occasion that one of our 'plumbers', as the armourers were called, was able to bring his 'secret weapon' into action. It had been the armourer sergeant's idea, some weeks earlier, to make up a fearsome looking weapon using what he had available. He and his men scrounged and stole a load of very robust pieces of angle iron from which they produced a very solid base to mount a weapon. Already in their possession were surplus machine-guns and boxes of .303 ammunition. With permission, they mounted the whole lot on their solid base which was in turn picketed to the ground. The boxes were kept fully loaded with ammunition of all types, ball, tracer and armour piercing. With four machine-guns securely attached, two rods were mounted to the unit for their shoulders to rest on and a hand grip either side completed the job.

On first observing the raid on St Merryn, the armourers quickly uncovered the weapon and made it ready for action. Having no previous opportunity to try it out, the sergeant was getting the feel of it, swinging it upwards, downwards, left and right in anticipation of actually getting to fire it!

His chance came when we saw one of the attacking aircraft, having dropped his bombs, finish his run and turn left instead of right as the others had done. Whatever he had spotted in our direction made him want to see more, and he headed straight for our dispersal. The German pilot finished his turn and lined up with our Spitfires – and that was when the armourers gave him all they had got.

The Brownings started firing and made one hell of a noise. We could see tracers heading off in the direction of the German raider. It certainly did all the sergeant said it would, but whether he hit the enemy or not I don't know, and the attacker turned away and disappeared out to sea. The weapon had proved its worth and justified the sergeant's request to build it. Needless to say, it was kept at readiness from then on.

After a couple of months at St Eval the 'gen' machine sniffed out a pending move. It was true and in the middle of August, the 14th, to be exact, the first line servicing groundcrew were air lifted to our new home at RAF Middle Wallop in Hampshire.

By the time Joe and the squadron had received news of their move, the Battle of Britain was well underway. The Luftwaffe's aim was to defeat the RAF in the air and on the ground. Raids were not just limited to the south-east of England and the Luftwaffe had been trying out the RAF defences up and down the coastline, from Scotland to Cornwall. Supply convoys had been a particular target in the English Channel as well as Radar stations and airfields. Middle Wallop was in 10 Group with a number of fighter squadrons resident.

Joe and his colleagues were flown up from St Eval in a slow, lumbering Handley Page Harrow. They landed, pretty much a sitting duck, in the middle of the day.

For me this was magic! I'd never flown before and as we filed aboard the Handley Page Harrow and occupied the plank-like seats running the full length of each side of the fuselage, quite a few of us could not conceal our excitement of our first flight. I can't remember being able to see out of the aircraft once we were airborne, but that didn't matter. It was all happening for us 19-year-olds and we loved it.

Even a message that came from up front that we were nearing Middle Wallop and that an air raid was in progress failed to dent our enthusiasm. The fact that we were told we would not be able to land made it all the more exciting for us groundcrew. Moments later we were advised that we would be dropping down to a very low height and head away from Middle Wallop until permission to return and land was received. It didn't seem that long before we landed safely on the grass at Middle Wallop – the airfield did not have tarmac runways at this point.

On reflection, I look back on this and think how stupid it was to try and move us by air into an area that was thick with prowling enemy Bf 109s. We were a sitting duck, easy prey for the 20mm cannon of those Yellow-nosed blighters! It sends a shiver down my spine now, but at the time I was young and eager, ready to hit the ground running and do our job.

Chapter 3

Hangar Catastrophe

Life No.8

Having jumped out of the Harrow in quite a hurry in case of any of the raiders returning, we were put aboard trucks and taken for a meal at the cookhouse on the main station. The plan was to feed us and then take us to dispersal to prepare for the arrival of our Spitfires.

There was another squadron of Spitfires there, 609 (West Riding) Squadron with the code letters 'PR'. Some of its groundcrew were there in the dining hall when we arrived. Having been there for some time prior to our arrival, they were the top dogs – and they didn't stop telling us so whilst we were consuming our bread and turnip jam sandwiches, all washed down with a huge mug of tea.

This sort of behaviour always went on when two squadrons met initially, but it was banter and nobody got hurt. I was just about to get another cup of tea when the siren went.

Having experienced air raids at Middle Wallop before, the 609 chaps leapt up and took off for the exits as fast as they could. Us of 234 Squadron, thinking 'what a shower', sat tight and made no effort to move. That was, as you might imagine, until all Hell broke loose outside. Then we went out pretty damn quick.

Not knowing the location of the air raid shelters or somewhere that was safe to head for, we could only watch from what little protection we found as the Luftwaffe bombed the Hell out of us. Building after building was blown apart, and hangars were smashed open – one even lost its main doors – as the relentless thud of exploding bombs seemed to go on and on.

From what I remember looking back on events, I think the first bomb detonated ahead of No.3 Hangar, while the second and third bombs fell directly between Nos. 4 and No.5 hangars, blowing out their windows and damaging the crash and fire tenders. The other bombs fell off to the right and exploded harmlessly on open ground. The bombs of another Ju 88 fell even further away and didn't seem to have much effect.

When it was all over, the airfield was a confused mixture of dust, smoke and people running and shouting while trying to help wherever possible. There was carnage everywhere, and we heard that three poor blokes who had tried to close the hangar doors during the raid had been squashed as they fell off their rails.

We set about trying to bring some sanity to the chaos that reigned. Eventually we were all rounded up and taken to the dispersals. At least we knew what to do the next time the sirens sounded.

The historian and author Chris Goss has extensively researched this attack on Middle Wallop. He provides the following information: 'The Ju 88s of Lehrgeschwader 1, led by Staffelkapitän Hauptmann Wilhelm Kern, reached Middle Wallop unchallenged. Kern then dived down to deliver three 250kg high-explosive, one 250kg incendiary and five 50kg fragmentation bombs upon the exposed airfield.

'The first bomb detonated ahead of No.3 Hangar, whilst the second and third bombs fell directly between Nos. 4 and 5 hangars, blowing out their windows and damaging the crash and fire tenders. The other bombs fell to the right and exploded harmlessly on open ground. The bombs of the second Ju 88 fell even further to the right. The third aircraft, flown by Oberleutnant Wilhelm Heinrici, saw what had happened to the bombs of his comrades and he took his Junkers down to less than 2,000 feet before releasing his.

'Walking over to the mess hall as the enemy appeared overhead were two pilots of 609 Squadron – Flying Officer Alexander Edge and Pilot Officer Eugene "Red" Tobin (an American who had only joined the squadron six days earlier). All around them airmen were throwing themselves to the ground. Edge started to run for cover, at which point Tobin called to him and they ran together, flinging themselves to the ground just as a Ju 88 released its deadly cargo. "My head was spinning," recalled Tobin, and "it felt as though I had a permanent ringing in my ears. I felt the blast go over me as I lay there flattened on the ground. I got up and my instinct was to run towards the hangar. It was carnage, I saw one overalled person with his foot and half a leg blown off, another had a great red patch on his chest with a load of mess hanging from it, another was rolling in agony with one of his arms missing. The door of the hangar was only half closed and just inside I could see the bodies of four overalled men on the ground with one seemingly splattered against the edge of the door. I felt sick, I almost threw up there and then, but as other air force personnel came into the hangar, they just seemed to go about their business in a respectable and calm manner with no sign of panic."'

Joe's further reflections on the events that day are just as sobering.

At the time the adrenalin was pumping. We were young, and we felt invincible. I don't think I had time to be scared. Up to that point I had not thought about death.

What I will tell you, though, is that you have never felt anything like the shock wave of a bomb going off. You felt it through your entire body, a complete sensory overload. I remember hearing and feeling the bomb going off through the ground and up through my chest. My ears were hurting badly; they rang for days after the explosion and I couldn't hear properly as I had a whistling noise like tinnitus.

The air was acrid with smoke from burning buildings, rubber, fuel. You could taste dust in your mouth and at times it was pretty shocking. I can't say I got used to it. I look back and now realise that I must have been scared, but we didn't show it, we had a job to do and we didn't want to let anyone down. We were not going to be the weak link in the chain. We had to keep the Spitfires in the air, if we didn't, we knew the consequences. We had heard the stories from the lads heading back from France that we had served with at St Eval.

One of the Spitfire pilots who witnessed the attack that day was Pilot Officer David Crook, who was serving on 609. Though David did not survive the war, he wrote about the attack in his book *Spitfire Pilot* which was published in 1942. I thought it would be worth including his comments here:

> 'After lunch the air-raid warning sounded and we dashed out of the mess and went down to the point where our Spitfires were. There were no orders for us to take off … so we sat in our aircraft and waited. A few minutes later we heard the unmistakable "oom-ooma" of a German bomber above the clouds. I immediately signalled to my ground crew to stand by, as I did not intend to sit on the ground and be bombed. I kept my finger on the engine starter button and waited expectantly.
>
> 'Almost immediately the enemy bomber, a Junkers 88, broke out of the cloud to the north of the aerodrome, turned slightly to get on his course and then dived at high speed towards the hangars. At about 1,500 feet he let go four bombs – we could see them very distinctly as they plunged down, and a second later there was an earth-shaking "whom" and four great clouds of dust arose. All this happened in a matter of seconds only, but by this time everybody had got their engines started and we all roared helter-skelter across the aerodrome.'

Leading Aircraftman Ernie Barker was also at Middle Wallop at the time, and his story shows a little of just what we groundcrew had to endure, not only during the attack but also in the aftermath. His account of his actions the following day has also been provided by Chris Goss with the permission of the 609 (West Riding) Squadron Archives:

> 'Ray Dunn and I had just finished our washing and shaving. We were in a barrack block, first floor … I looked out of the window and noticed 3 army chaps, one digging furiously with a pick, another one was shovelling all the soil away, and the third chap was just standing there. I called over to Ray to come and have a look and we decided that the three blokes were digging some sort of drain, perhaps to enhance our environment, perhaps not. However I remember both Ray and I shouting at them such phrases as "up your pipe" and "get lost" and other popular euphemisms of the day.
>
> 'The soldier who we dubbed as the quiet one, because he didn't appear to be doing any work, came striding towards us and stopped just below our window, and it was only then that we noticed his rank on his shoulder tabs … a major! "Oh hell, this is it," I thought, and before I could think anymore the major screamed at us, using such words that I had never heard before (but I did discover later on in life that I too could make myself better understood by using these words). From his verbal tirade of words and phrases I could just about make out that he was ordering us to come down to him immediately – if not before.
>
> 'This we did of course, and for the next ten minutes he lectured us on the meaning of tannoy messages broadcast all over the station, including dispersal points, for all personnel. I muttered meekly that I had heard the tannoy mentioning something about evacuating all barrack blocks for that afternoon, but I thought "Well, that didn't really mean me"; how stupid we were at eighteen years old!

'After more fuming on the major's part, he told us to follow him to the spot where the other two army blokes were still digging and shovelling. I looked down into the pit they were digging, and my first thought was that they were digging a grave, but then I saw IT, an unexploded bomb!

'The major told his men to come out of the pit for a rest, and somehow or other I thought this is going to be painful. I thought about doing a hasty retreat and run as fast as possible, but then I said to myself "You coward Ernie, what would Mr Churchill say!" I was brought back to reality by the piercing voice of the major, and looking me straight in the eye he ordered me to pick up a pick, get down in the trench, and start digging underneath the bomb. I nearly died of fright, but I did jump into the pit (or was I pushed!).

'The pit was quite small, about 4 feet down and a couple of feet across. The bomb was lying at an angle of about 45 degrees and it was no easy task to get the pick directly underneath it without touching the damn thing. Well, I picked gingerly, about an inch at a time, and the major, being no fool, noticed that I was hardly working flat out. He tried to instil into me that there was a very strong possibility that the bomb could explode any second, indeed if I noticed a hissing noise then that would be the sign that an explosion was imminent, there would not even be time for all my past life to pass before me. The bomb was a 250lb one, and although the major repeated time and time again that it was a delayed action type, I chose to repeat to myself a million times that he was lying and that it really was just a dud bomb. How I could think on those lines I will never know because at that time I knew very little about German bombs, in fact I knew absolutely nothing!

'However, after doing my stint in the pit, the major ordered me out and it was then that I thought I heard the damn thing hissing. Unfortunately I did not have the opportunity to come out because the major threw himself into the pit taking me with him. He put his arm underneath the bomb and told everybody to be absolutely still. I cannot describe my feelings at the time, I had already sweated profusely, but now sweat poured out of me, my legs started to dither and I could hardly breathe. This was it I thought, at least it will be all over rather quickly, wouldn't feel a thing.

'The quietness period ordered by the major lasted for hours, or so it seemed, but in fact it only lasted for about 30 seconds. He jumped out of the pit, ordered me out, and then sent Ray in to do more digging. He was eventually ordered out, more unkind words from the major and we were dismissed. Ray and I casually ran back to the barrack block, but before entering we agreed that perhaps it would not be the correct thing to do, so we beat a hasty retreat over to dispersal. Nothing was reported about this incident, at least I don't think it was. Ray and I both agreed that we had got off lightly.'

No.234 Squadron's Spitfires were soon in action the following day when another raid developed over Middle Wallop. Bombs or not, Joe and the other groundcrew were still expected to don their tin hats and get on with turning their aircraft around to ensure the squadron was at readiness.

This time, twelve bombs were dropped and mostly fell wide, though two hangars were hit. One aircraft was destroyed and five more damaged, but luckily no casualties.

We weaved our way around the perimeter of the airfield to avoid being caught out in the open if any raiders should return. We arrived at our dispersal at the bottom of the airfield which had a few tents, a couple of marquees and some small wooden huts. To add insult to injury, it was within spitting distance of the bomb dump. Not to worry, we set about preparing to receive our aircraft and bring them to readiness standard.

Full 500-gallon petrol bowsers were there, along with everything we would require. When the pilots returned, we each received our own aircraft as it taxied in. The fitters and riggers stood waving their arms to guide in their pilots to where they would park ready to be worked on.

Before the pilot was even out of his cockpit, the bowser would pull up and the fitter there begin the process of filling up the fuel tank. All trades were now swarming over their aircraft like a lot of ants, putting to use all the skills they had learned and practised for hours on end at Church Fenton.

The aircraft were soon ready, with fuel, oil, air, glycol, oxygen and ammo all replenished. After flight inspections had been completed by all trades, each Spitfire now stood ready

A brave cameraman captured this photograph of the moment that one of the German bombs exploded as the raid on Middle Wallop got underway on 14 August 1940. (*Chris Goss*)

at dispersal, the starter battery plugged in with chocks in position, ropes outwards. These were stretched out ready for a quick removal when we were scrambled.

Each aircraft had its own paperwork called a 'Form 700'. These had to be signed by all tradesmen to show that his part of the job had been completed. The whole lot was then countersigned by the senior non-commissioned officer in charge of each flight.

It was now the responsibility of the fitter (engine) and rigger (airframe) on their assigned aircraft to make final preparations, depending on the state of readiness the squadron was at, this being dictated by Operations. All other trades, their respective jobs completed on the aircraft for now, would be attending to the requirements of their trade and begin getting these ready for their Spitfire's next sortie.

Members of 609 (West Riding) Squadron's groundcrew seek shelter during the attack on 14 August 1940. (*Chris Goss*)

The shell of Middle Wallop's No.5 Hangar. The large steel door that caused three of the deaths during the attack on 14 August 1940, can be seen lying on the ground. (*Chris Goss*)

Looking out from No.5 Hangar at the large steel door that had been blown from its runners by a direct hit on the structure. A few days after the devastating attack, on 23 August 1940, Middle Wallop was visited by HRH the Duke of Kent. (*Chris Goss*)

The 609 Squadron Operations Record entry for 14 August 1940, includes the following: 'Middle Wallop Station was raided by three twin-engined enemy bombers, who scored hits on our hangar, and made a shambles of the Offices'. The damage seen here was to the airfield's Orderly Room. (*Chris Goss*)

One of Middle Wallop's damaged hangars after the attack on 14 August 1940. The airborne interception aerials are just about visible on the wing of the 604 (County of London) Squadron Blenheim. (*Chris Goss*)

The pitiful remains of a 609 (West Riding) Squadron Spitfire pictured after the events of 14 August 1940. (*Chris Goss*)

A large crater marks a near miss for one of the hangars at Middle Wallop. (*Chris Goss*)

Bullets or bomb fragments left their mark on this building at Middle Wallop. (*Chris Goss*)

Another of the many craters that the Ju 88s of *Lehrgeschwader* 1 left scattered across Middle Wallop on 14 August 1940. (*Chris Goss*)

Members of groundcrew called together and about to start work clearing up the damage at Middle Wallop in the aftermath of *Lehrgeschwader* 1's attack. (*Chris Goss*)

The wreckage of a Blenheim at Middle Wallop in the aftermath of the attack on 14 August 1940. (*Chris Goss*)

Groundcrew and station personnel make their way through a badly battered RAF Middle Wallop following the events of 14 August 1940. (*Chris Goss*)

Once again a plume of smoke rises over RAF Middle Wallop as a German bomb explodes – though this time whilst bomb disposal personnel deal with the unexploded bombs left over from the attack on 14 August 1940. Note the camouflage applied to many of the buildings. (*Chris Goss*)

An image that reveals a small part of the damage that the German bombers wrought on RAF Middle Wallop on 14 August 1940. (*Chris Goss*)

Groundcrew go about their duties at Middle Wallop as another unexploded bomb is destroyed in a controlled explosion. (*Chris Goss*)

The inside of one of Middle Wallop's hangars pictured after the raiders had departed on 14 August 1940. (*Chris Goss*)

Chapter 4

Attack on the Fuel Bowser

Life No.7

There is another incident that I was involved in at Middle Wallop which I still remember vividly, despite the fact that it was a long time ago.

We had to maintain full petrol tankers at dispersal. We were getting low on one of the 500 gallon bowsers that we towed by tractors, and, as the Spitfires would require re-fuelling on their return, I was despatched to top it up. I set off driving the tractor with the tanker in tow to go to the fuel dump at the main camp to get filled up.

I headed across the airfield in a straight line. However, on arrival I found the place unmanned and everything locked up.

I had to fill this tanker, so I parked it alongside the 100 octane petrol pump and went on a hunt for the keys. Fortunately, they were all on a board in the office and having grabbed the bunch I needed I went out and filled up the bowser. Having replaced the keys, I duly started my return journey to the dispersal.

This time I stayed within about fifty yards of the edge of the airfield. Before reaching halfway, the siren sounded. Within minutes a raid was in progress. I could hear explosions on the main camp, but I pressed on until the sound of an aircraft approaching from my right caused me to look in that direction.

At this point a Heinkel He 111, flying very low, released its bombs and they appeared to be heading my way! I threw the tractor in to neutral, leapt off and set off as fast as I could go towards the airfield's boundary hedge.

I just ran and ran until completely out of breath, at which point I then sank down. Placing my hands over my head, I buried my face in the grass.

I heard explosions in the main camp and looked up to see where the aircraft was, but there was not one in sight. I ran back to the tractor and set off again for the dispersal. I made it ok no problems, no comments – we had our fuel.

Had the He 111 scored a direct hit on the full fuel bowser it would have meant certain death for Joe. He was always very matter of fact about this incident, saying that he had to do the job in hand otherwise the pilots couldn't have got back into the action. He would often recall the sound of the dropping bombs and the deafening explosions vibrating the ground, shaking his body and how long after he suffered with ringing in his ears.

The attack that very nearly blew Joe to smithereens was probably that which occurred on 15 August 1940. Few would doubt that RAF groundcrew at this stage of the Battle of Britain

Aircraftman 'Smudge' Smith posing in the cockpit of a 234 Squadron Spitfire Mk.I, coded 'AZ-Q', at Middle Wallop. Note how he has picked up the pilot's B-Type flying helmet off the seat and is holding it in his left hand. According to Bob, this is thought to have been X4009, which was the aircraft regularly flown by 22-year-old Australian Acting Flight Lieutenant Paterson Clarence 'Pat' Hughes DFC. X4009 arrived on the squadron on 19 August 1940. Joe stated that he regularly looked after this aircraft, alongside that of Bob Doe. However, it is worth noting that Hughes was the 'B' Flight commander, not 'A' Flight. (*Mark Hillier Collection*)

Aircraftman Clements, an armourer in 234 Squadron, impersonates a pilot in the cockpit of 'AZ-Q' at Middle Wallop in 1940. Clements is wearing a pilot's B-Type leather flying helmet and Mk.IIIa goggles. Note also what appears to be a rear-view mirror added to the side of the canopy frame above his head. This aircraft was lost on 7 September 1940, when Hughes was seen to ram a Dornier Do 17 – eyewitnesses state that this was a deliberate act – which then crashed to earth at a waterworks at Darks Farm, Bessels Green. The Spitfire fell in a field at Sundridge. Pat's body, parachute unopened, fell in the back garden of a bungalow 100 yards away. The Australian's inseparable companion, an Airedale Terrier named Butch, was never seen again after his master's loss, and it is widely believed that he had accompanied him on his last flight. (*Mark Hillier Collection*)

were very much in the front line. Armourer Fred Roberts was serving in 12 Group when he had similar experiences to Joe. His account of being under fire comes from his excellent book Duxford to Karachi *(Victory Press, Worcester, 2006):*

'At about 08:30 hrs, while the Squadron was away, I was in the breakfast queue at Fowlmere, knife, fork, spoon and enamel plate in hand. The village air raid siren had sounded an imminent air raid warning when someone shouted, "They're nearly overhead!"

'Looking up I could see these planes which I learned later were Dornier 17s. There were about 30 of them. I could see them shining in the sun. I could also see the bombs dropping! A quick dive into the nearby slit trench along with the others and I remember sitting there holding my enamel plate over my head. I don't know what protection it would have given.

Another photograph of Aircraftman Clements in the cockpit of 'AZ-Q'. Note the artwork on the side of the cockpit, 'A' Flight's emblem, and what appears to be the inscription 'Dodger II', although it's not that clear. (*Mark Hillier Collection*)

'Fortunately for us the bombs had been released late, only one bomb landing on the airfield and this among our bell tents. It exploded, making a crater four-foot-deep and five foot across. A second bomb exploded just beyond the boundary fence, and a few more in the nearby orchards and watercress beds. We had no casualties, but John and Jimmy Belton were still in bed and had the tent they were in blown on top of them; they were half buried with earth from the bomb crater.'

The Luftwaffe did not have it all its own way in these attacks, with both 234 and 609 squadrons making a number of claims. No.609 claimed forty-four kills in August alone for the loss of twenty-six Spitfires through combat or accidents. Likewise, 234 Squadron's achievements in the Battle of Britain were significant – fifteen of its pilots had shared a total of seventy-two enemy aircraft destroyed, probable or damaged. Joe and his fellow groundcrew were instrumental in that success, keeping all the aircraft fuelled armed and ready for action.

We were there the day that 609 Squadron shot down its 100th enemy aircraft. Their pilots had retrieved parachutes from the downed bomber crew, and they had had scarves made from them, dyed different colours.

Everybody worked long and hard those days. We would have the aircraft available for whatever readiness state the squadron was given by dawn, or a time that could be as early as 2.45 a.m. The last flight of the day could be landing at dusk or 10 p.m in August. And then we would have one or two hours work on the aircraft

Aircraftman Clements standing in front of 'AZ-Q' at dispersal, RAF Middle Wallop, in August 1940. (*Mark Hillier Collection*)

It was through the production of the TV programme *Spitfire Ace* by RDF media that Bob Doe and Joe renewed their acquaintance. Joe would visit Bob and his wife Betty at his home in East Sussex and they remained in contact right up to Bob's death. Joe stayed in touch with Betty until he himself passed away in 2017. (*Mark Hillier Collection*)

depending on the state they returned after combat. We had to get them ready for the next day.

The weather was pretty good most days and once the aircraft were away, we could snatch a nap or any other times that were available to get forty winks. There was no complaining, moaning or groaning. Everybody wanted our squadron to be the best. For much of the summer there were no days off – our main aim was just to keep the aircraft serviceable.

The ground crews were proud of their individual aircraft and very competitive. Often the same pilot would fly your aircraft regularly and the same pride and loyalty existed. Your aircraft was the best, your pilot was the best and everything was maintained to the highest standard. We had our favourites naturally. Some of the names I can remember are Pilot Officer Bob Doe, one of our top scoring pilots, and our flight commander, Flight Lieutenant Pat Hughes. An Australian with his Navy blue uniform, Pat was very

Pilot Officer Bob Doe wearing his Mae West and holding his B-Type flying helmet next to his Spitfire at Middle Wallop. (*Mark Hillier Collection*)

Paterson Clarence Hughes pictured relaxing at dispersal in his dark blue RAAF uniform. Joe Roddis was often the fitter working on Pat's aircraft. (*Courtesy of the Battle of Britain London Monument*)

In 2013, Joe attended a book signing event at the Shoreham Aircraft Museum along with two other Battle of Britain veterans, Wing Commander Tom Neil DFC & Bar and Squadron Leader Nigel Rose. Shoreham had remains of both Pat Hughes' Spitfire and the Dornier that he rammed on display. Joe took the photos he had of 'AZ-Q' with him to show the museum staff. After the signing Joe was taken by his co-author to the spot where the museum had recently unveiled a memorial stone to Pat close to where he had fallen. It was a very emotional day for Joe, bringing back the summer days of 1940 and his last memories of his pilot. (*Mark Hillier Collection*)

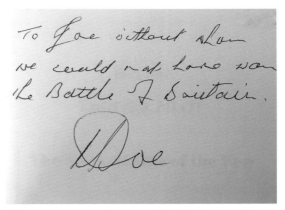

The inscription inside a copy of Bob Doe's memoirs that he sent to Joe. (*Mark Hillier Collection*)

much liked and respected. He was sadly lost one day when leading his flight over London against huge odds!

We got a bit of a mauling at Middle Wallop. We arrived with twenty-one fully experienced pilots, but by the middle of September we were down to three of the originals. Our replacements, having virtually no experience, were being shot down in a very short space of time. My pilot at that stage was one of the three originals, Bob Doe, who normally flew Spitfire AZ-D.

Bob was an absolute gent. He had no airs and graces and treated us fairly, he always spoke to us and we respected him. In his memoirs

Bob wrote that, 'The camaraderie between the troops and ourselves was very close. No one saluted anyone at dispersal, but everything got done.' Bob became the third-highest scoring pilot in the Battle of Britain.

Flight Lieutenant Paterson Clarence Hughes was originally in the Royal Australian Air Force but transferred to the RAF. He distinguished himself in the Battle of Britain and was later awarded the DFC. He was chasing a Dornier Do 17 over Kent on 7 September 1940, when he was either hit by wreckage from the bomber or possibly hit by friendly fire. He parachuted out, but his chute did not open, and he was sadly killed.

We also had two Polish Sergeant pilots – 'Ziggy' Klein and Jan Zurakowski. They were only ever really happy when in the air shooting Germans down – and they were good at it. We called them Zig and Zag, they spoke little English and their names were not too easy to say. There were many more, but you couldn't get to know all the pilots.

Janusz Zurakowski went on to become a well-known test pilot. He was born at Ryzawka, Eastern Poland, on 12 September 1914. He joined the Polish Air Force at Deblin in 1934. Following the invasion of his country in 1939, Zurakowski reached the UK later that year. Commissioned in the RAFVR in January 1940, he was posted to the Polish Wing at 3 School of Technical Training Blackpool.

Sent for initial grading and testing at 15 EFTS Redhill in July he was then sent to 5 OTU Aston Down and converted to Spitfires. Initially posted to 152 Squadron at Warmwell, Zurakowski was then posted to 234 Squadron at St. Eval. He flew his first operational sortie on 15 August 1940, after the move to Middle Wallop, during which he destroyed a Me 110.

Zurakowski was shot down in Spitfire N3239 on 24 August, the victor being either Oberstleutnant Hans Karl Meyer of 1 Lehrgeschwader 53 or Leutnant A. Zeiss of Staffel Jagdgeschwader 53, or, indeed, a combination of them both. He crashed on the Isle of Wight in Spitfire N3239, thankfully unhurt. Zurakowski was recorded as officially killed, much to his surprise when he returned to the squadron the following day. He received two letters marked 'Killed in action' and in some accounts this is still claimed.

He had further success on 5 September 1940, when he destroyed a Me109, followed by another the following day. In this later action Zurakowski's Spitfire, N3279, was damaged by a Me 109 over Beachy Head and he crashed on landing back at Middle Wallop. This Joe remembered as being quite spectacular.

Clearly the Spitfire had been damaged. We could see Zurakowski's aircraft approaching the field, but the wheels were only partly down. This was not a good situation and it was clear that the aircraft would possibly dig in and nose over. This was not great as the residual fuel could rupture from the fuel tank and catch fire! Also getting the pilot out of the cockpit would be extremely hard if the wreck was on fire, or we could make any injuries worse if he had been wounded in combat.

He slowed right down. The flaps came down and we held our breath. Crash, bang, wallop – he hit hard, and the Spitfire's nose dug in as we thought it would. The aircraft rose up and went tail over nose. Amazingly, he walked away from it, albeit looking a bit dazed! The underside was peppered with cannon shell holes. A lucky escape indeed.

Zurakowski was to later share in the probable destruction of a Me 110 on 29 September 1940. He was posted to 609 (West Riding) Squadron, also at Middle Wallop, on 4 October.

Over the days and weeks we were at Middle Wallop you'd likely see all the pilots take off at some time or another, and then seen them return – but not always. To us, our pilots earned everything we could do for them. We had the utmost respect for them. We would see the damage they came back with and it made you wince a bit and think about how you were going to get them back up again.

When the 'Jerrys' came, we got them airborne then dived for the slit trench. The pilots went out to take them on and often paid the ultimate price. It was clear from the damage that the Luftwaffe had a clear advantage in the 20mm cannon compared to our .303 rounds.

As for the aforementioned slit trenches, as there were no air raid shelters at the dispersal, the first thing we did after settling in was to dig a damn great slit trench in the solid chalk. If you were at the far end of the flight line and the siren went, it was up to you to find shelter before the Ju 87s or whatever fell upon us. If you were lucky enough to be in the vicinity of a trench, in you dived, usually on top of the quicker runners or those that had been nearer.

The day we blessed ever having dug a trench so deep and long will be remembered by all of the 234 Squadron groundcrew who were with us at that time. We'd been brought to full readiness, but not scrambled. Pilots were in cockpits, groundcrews ready for a quick start-up and still they held us on the ground.

Directly above us, pretty high up, were hordes of Me 109s just circling round and round, but doing nothing threatening. Everyone was watching this show above us when they suddenly stopped circling and headed off for Southampton.

SCRAMBLE! Red Verey lights peppered the sky and off the squadron went, closely followed by 609, the whole lot climbing up to get the 109s. We watched for a short while in the silence that followed and then we became aware of why they had enticed our Spitfires away.

Ju 87s that had been out of sight above the 109s started diving down and soon bombs were falling towards the main camp again. We didn't stop to count them, just headed at top speed for the slit trench. I dived in and crouched there listening to the diving Stukas and the crash of their bombs flattening buildings.

You could see the bombs leave the Stuka at the end of its dive hoping that it wasn't meant for us. We had our secret weapon fixed up by the slit trench, but it would not have been a good idea to attract attention of the Stukas and bring them our way.

Bob Doe recalled that this secret weapon was put into play on occasion: 'I remember that some of the armourers started taking a more active part in the war by building their own ack- ack defences. They mounted four browning guns on a railway sleeper and set the contraption up on a hummock, just behind the dispersal hut. Where the stuff come from we didn't ask, but during the next raid they manned their gun and succeeded in putting a bullet through our hut! With their honour satisfied and our nerves in ruins, we invited them to remove it and join us in the dugout.'

Life at Middle Wallop in the summer of 1940 was hectic to say the least, but it was exciting to us and we were being paid to do it. Occasionally, due to bad weather or as a relaxing of the raids on our airfields by the Luftwaffe, command would stand the squadron down and once all aircraft were fully serviceable, the flight sergeant in charge would give us time off to catch up on sleep, laundry and personal jobs, but we were not allowed to leave the camp. During one month at Middle Wallop I don't ever recall leaving the camp, although some of the pilots and ground crew say they found a good pub in Nether Wallop.

We lost pilots, we lost Spitfires, and, on the squadron's return, if your Spitfire was not home you started asking questions. Had the pilot been able to bale out? Was he safe? Had he been injured, and would he be returning to fly with us? Losses were sadly becoming commonplace. You felt that loss as a squadron, but you had to pull together and get on with it. We could see what these chaps could do, and we were proud to be part of the team.

When your Spitfire landed after a scramble, the pilot would report any problems attributed to unserviceability. He would enter the details on the Form 700 and every attempt to rectify them would be made by us first line servicing crews. The flight sergeant in charge would sort out which problems could be resolved quickly, and which would require second line service rectification.

Our after-flight inspection would require laid down checks on the aircraft, including refuelling etc., but also a close visual inspection of the whole aircraft. Bullet holes in cowlings meant removal to see what internal damage had been inflicted. Bullet holes in the propeller blades would be closely examined, and if not serious would just be filed smooth and let go. Common sense prevailed.

By 11 September 1940, the squadron headed back to St Eval. We were rightly proud of our involvement in the work of Nos. 10 and 11 Groups. We had played our part and now we were off home to a less hectic job of work.

We soon settled into our routine and nothing or very little seemed to have changed during our time away. There were some signs of being visited by the Luftwaffe occasionally, but having seen the damage inflicted on Middle Wallop and other fighter airfields along the South Coast, it could be best described as slight.

The accommodation and the station showed signs of some light bombing, but we called them nuisance raids. The two changes that did directly affect us were that we were on a different dispersal, and shortly after our arrival we were moved off camp to live in Newquay. The accommodation on camp, the wooden billets we had previously occupied, were apparently now considered unfit for use.

I don't know what the aircrew billeting situation was, but the groundcrew were all billeted in various large houses near to Newquay. I was in a house at Watergate Bay, the rear garden of which led down to the beach. It was a wonderful place to be billeted and about thirty of us were very happy there.

We were bussed to and from the airfield each day, about thirty minutes run, maybe more. Our new dispersal was at the opposite side to where we had been previously. We were kept busy all day every day, but not at the frantic pitch we had maintained up at Middle Wallop. I don't remember what ops the pilots were doing now but they did see a considerable amount of action!

One morning, on our arrival at dispersal we saw three strange aircraft parked near to our Spitfires. They turned out to be Westland Whirlwinds which had the code letters 'HE' of 263 Squadron. They had two Rolls-Royce Peregrine engines and a lovely complete tool kit in the engine nacelle. There didn't appear to be any of their groundcrew with them, so I was assigned to one of the Whirlwinds just to keep an eye on it and be available with a rigger to start it up if and when they left.

The story was that they'd come to St Eval to deal with the Focke-Wulf Fw 200 Condors that were causing problems to the Atlantic convoys. They had four vicious looking cannon in the nose, were twin engine and had a high tailplane. This would enable them to reach high altitude quickly and then they had the armament to deal with the big German bombers. However, they never did anything while at St Eval and one day they just started up and flew away.

We lost our first groundcrew member at St Eval. One night this young airman, an 18-year-old called Browning, was on guard duty when the air raid warning went. He went into the shelter with others, but it received a direct hit and they were all killed.

Chapter 5

Near Miss With a Propeller

Life No.6

I left 234 Squadron early in March 1941 to travel north to my native Yorkshire where I had been ordered to join another Spitfire squadron at RAF Driffield. No.485 (NZ) Squadron was just being formed with New Zealand aircrew and RAF groundcrew.

After arrival and with formalities dealt with, I was put on 'A' Flight and allocated a Spitfire which had the code letters 'OU-F' and the serial number X4621. It was a Mk.I which was named *Martyn Evans Bevan*. The rigger on the plane responsible for airframe servicing was Danny McWhinnie from Musselburgh, near Edinburgh, and I was the engine man.

The aircraft that Joe was first allocated on his new squadron was a presentation Spitfire, purchased with a donation of £6,000 by a Mr D.M. Evans of 'Danycraig'. Newton Porthcawl, South Wales. and was named after his son. It had previously served with 19 Squadron at RAF Fowlmere in closing stages of the Battle of Britain.

William Vernon Crawford-Compton was a founding member of 234 Squadron. He became one of its most successful aces. By the end of the war he had twenty-one confirmed victories and had been awarded a DSO and Bar and DFC and Bar. He remained in the RAF post-war, achieving the rank of Air Vice-Marshal before retiring in 1969.

The newly-created 485 was not the first New Zealand squadron, that honour went to 75 (NZ) Squadron, a bomber unit equipped with Vickers Wellingtons that had been formed in 1940. No.485 (NZ) Squadron was, however, the first fighter unit. In total, seven New Zealand squadrons were formed during the Second World War under the control of the RAF, three of which were in Fighter Command. No.485's first commanding officer was the 28-year-old New Zealander Squadron Leader Marcus Knight.

Some of the pilots posted to help form the fledgling unit had flown during the Battle of Britain. That said, one of the squadrons founder members and a new, inexperienced pilot, was Sergeant William Vernon Crawford-Compton, who, in time, became one of the squadron's most successful aces.

Crawford-Compton, wearing a Mae West, is pictured here standing on the wing of his 485 Squadron Spitfire at RAF Station Kenley. (*Air Force Museum of New Zealand/Public Domain*)

A group of 485 Squadron's pilots walking away from a Spitfire at RAF Driffield – leaving their aircraft to be worked on by the groundcrew. (*Air Force Museum of New Zealand/Public Domain*)

This group photograph is believed to show the founding pilots of 485 (NZ) Squadron, and some of their groundcrew, in front of a Spitfire at RAF Driffield. (*Air Force Museum of New Zealand/Public Domain*)

By the end of the war Crawford-Compton had twenty-one confirmed victories and was awarded a DSO and Bar and the DFC and Bar, as well as the American Silver Star, Légion d'Honneur and Croix de Guerre avec Palme. He remained in the RAF post-war and was awarded a CB and CBE, achieving Air Vice-Marshal rank before retiring in 1969.

Soon after my arrival, the squadron, along with its Mk.I Spitfires, moved a few miles north to RAF Leconfield, where it soon converted to Mk.IIa Spitfires. Whilst there we soon got into the busy routine of flying and training to bring the squadron up to the required standard for our future role in the war.

The first pilot I recall taking over and flying 'OU-F' was Sergeant Reginald Grant. He had been posted in from 145 Squadron, where he had already earned the Distinguished Flying Medal. He was later to become the commanding officer. Flying Officer Edward 'Hawkeye' Wells also flew our aircraft; he, too, was later to become CO of the unit!

It was all pretty routine stuff during this period and quite tame after 234 Squadron and the Battle of Britain. We still saw our fair share of action and bombing locally, but the squadron was not directly involved as we were still working up to become operational.

The outstanding difference the groundcrew noticed and often commented on while with 485 (NZ) Squadron was the much more sociable and relaxed atmosphere that existed between the New Zealand aircrew and we groundcrew. We were made to feel part of the team and not just an 'erk'.

It was at Leconfield that we got our first contingent of New Zealand groundcrew. They arrived late one evening led by Leading Aircraftsman Ernie Bongard, who was an armourer. They consisted of about half-a-dozen men, comprising both armourers and wireless tradesmen. They looked at the time of arrival as if they had walked all the way from New Zealand. They were tired and dirty from travelling. At that stage we were working some pretty gruesome hours, a fact that didn't cheer them up in the slightest!

Early morning readiness meant being at your aircraft by 3 a.m. and we didn't stand down at the end of the day until all the aircraft were serviceable and ready for the next day's operations. This could often be around midnight.

The nearby port of Hull was taking a lot of stick from the Luftwaffe and we didn't want any strays on our dispersal, so we pushed our Spitfires in to adjacent fields for safety. The next morning at 3 a.m. we would push them back to begin the pre-flight inspections and prepare them for flying. This went on for some time, but there were very seldom any moans and groans.

When Hull did get a raid, usually at night, we'd be issued with rifles to try and shoot out the parachute flares if they appeared to be drifting over in the direction of the airfield.

No.234 Squadron's football team at RAF Leconfield in 1942. In the back row, left to right, are Bert Ryman, Shaby, Yorky, Wilkie, Vic Strange, and Jock. While in the front row, again left to right, are Paddy, Joe, Butch, Dun, and Tony. (*Mark Hillier Collection*)

The squadron work up was being undertaken within the relative safety of 13 Group. Fortunately, as some of the pilots had previous combat experience, training went well and soon 485 was undertaking shipping patrols. The squadron soon had its first encounters with enemy aircraft, resulting in the first victory for the squadron. This honour went to Squadron Leader Knight, who claimed a Ju 88 on 2 June 1941. However, as Joe recalled, this key milestone was followed a couple of weeks later by tragedy.

One of my earliest and most vivid memories of being with 485 Squadron was a sad one – the squadron's first fatal flying accident. One of the pilots, Sergeant Kevin Cox, had a younger brother in the Royal New Zealand Navy and when his ship docked in England, he got leave to visit him.

After a conducted tour of the squadron and introductions all round, Kevin took off in a Spitfire to give a flying display. With us all watching he gave a good show, ending it with a low pass, inverted and at about 500 feet.

Every man watching knew he was too low and too slow. Whether he tried to right the aircraft, or it stalled, we shall never know, but he just dived straight into the field by the side of the cafe and stuck in the ground like a dart at 45 degrees.

We all rushed over to see what could be done, but couldn't get within fifty feet because of the flames and smoke, as well as the fact that the air was full of exploding ammunition. The intensity of the flames was such that we were all driven back and could feel the hairs on our arms and faces singe – but we desperately wanted to help the poor lad trapped inside.

We could see the pilot slumped in the cockpit and all his brother could do was stand and watch. It turned out there was probably nothing we could have done even if we had been able to get to him. When the station fire crew arrived and got the fire out, they took the canopy off, but it was discovered that the control column had gone right through his chest.

The feeling of utter helplessness and horror which we all experienced that day never really left. I would suffer many nightmares about that event.

Originating from Hamilton, New Zealand, Sergeant Kevin Desmond Cox RNZAF was aged just 20 when he killed at the controls of Spitfire P7758. He was buried at Leconfield Churchyard.

From Leconfield, I went off to do an engine fitters' course at RAF St Athan in Wales. Unlike a lot of others I knew who made the conversion from mechanic to fitter only to be posted to a different unit, on successful completion of this I was fortunate to have re-joined 485.

After about three months, the squadron moved south to Redhill in Surrey. By now, July 1941, we were beginning to resemble a competent well organised unit. The luxury of permanent RAF station facilities was left behind and we began to feel we were on active service. It was at Redhill that we exchanged our Mk.IIa Spitfires for Mk.VBs in August 1941.

Redhill was a pleasant little airfield and at our dispersal over on the far side we were next to a small lane that lead to the village. Across the lane was a large house that had a

Some of 485 (NZ) Squadron's Mk.V Spitfires at Redhill in the summer of 1941. The aircraft closest to the camera is 'OU-C'. With the serial number W3528, this Spitfire was flown by Sergeant Lyndon 'Lyn' Griffith. W3528 was a presentation aircraft, that had been paid for by funds raised by the Women's Division of the Farmers Union of New Zealand. Lyn claimed a Me 109 damaged in this aircraft on 13 October 1941, during Circus 108A. Reg Grant, who later went on to become the Commanding Officer of 485, also claimed a Me 109 and Fw 190 destroyed and one probable in this particular aircraft while flying from Kenley.

Spitfire Mk.V 'OU-U' pictured at Redhill. With the serial number BM155, it was regularly flown by Sergeant A.R. Robson. He claimed one Fw 190 destroyed, two aircraft probable, and one more damaged whilst flying this Spitfire. (*WW2 images*)

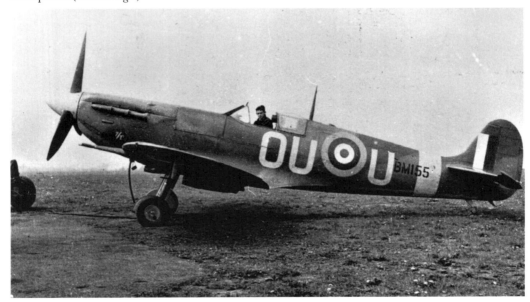

couple of rooms converted into a cafe and it did a good trade, albeit in competition with the daily visits by the NAAFI van.

From early 1941, we began to increasingly go on the offensive across the Channel, engaging in both fighter sweeps and bomber escort duties. These operations were known by various codenames, all strange names, such as *Circus* (bomber sorties heavily escorted by fighters in an effort to entice the Luftwaffe up into action), *Ramrod* (fighters escorting bombers to destroy a target), *Rhubarb* (free-lance fighter sorties), *Rodeo* (fighter sweeps), and *Sweep* (offensive flight by fighters to draw up the enemy).

The squadron was to see its fair share of successes and losses whilst at Redhill. Of the latter, Sergeant William Hendry, Pilot Officer Charles Stewart, Sergeant Jack Maney, Sergeant Vic Goodwin, Sergeant Bill Russell, Sergeant George Porter, Sergeant Keith Miller, Pilot Officer Bill Middleton, Sergeant Ian Paget, and Pilot Officer John Knight were all posted missing during this period. It was later reported that Russell and Knight were prisoners of war.

Such was the gathering pace of operations that aircraft often returned damaged or with injured pilots. The groundcrew were kept busy repairing and making good any battle damage ready for the next sortie. There were no real luxuries at Redhill and the accommodation was fairly basic, with the groundcrew accommodated in Nissen huts.

Ground crew re-arming a 485 (NZ) Squadron Spitfire on 22 July 1941, on which date the unit was at RAF Redhill. Pictured on the wing, left to right, are Leading Aircraftman Erridge and Leading Aircraftman A.W. Martin. Meanwhile, under the wing are Leading Aircraftman McGibbon, Leading Aircraftman Ernie Bongard, and Aircraftman 1st Class J.B. Neville. Joe recalls that Bongard, an armourer, was one of the first New Zealand groundcrew to join the squadron. (*Air Force Museum of New Zealand/Public Domain*)

One of 485 Squadron's groundcrew adding artwork to one of the squadron's Spitfires in 1941. As well as the personal emblem of a rampant lion on a shield with the legend 'Peggy – Per Angusta – As Augusta', there is also the name of this presentation aircraft, *Auckland V (Remuera)*. (*Air Force Museum of New Zealand/Public Domain*)

One of Joe's 485 Squadron groundcrew colleagues pictured in the cockpit of Spitfire AB870, which, a presentation aircraft coded 'OU-Z', was the regular mount of Squadron Leader M.W.B. Knight. Note the Squadron Leader's pennant on the side of the cockpit. (*Air Force Museum of New Zealand/Public Domain*)

By October 1941 we were on the move again. This time by road and rail to RAF Kenley, not that far away and still in Surrey. A pre-war RAF station, Kenley was luxury compared to Redhill, with a pub just within walking distance of the boundary fence and Whyteleafe close by, and Croydon not that further away. There we occupied the RAF married quarters and about six of us shared a room.

An autographed image of some of the 485 (NZ) Squadron pilots who had flown during the 'Channel Dash'. In the front row, left to right, are Harvey Sweetman, Dave Clouston, Reg 'Dumbo' Grant, Edward 'Hawkeye' Wells, Bill Crawford-Compton, Johnny Checketts and Reg Baker. Behind them, also left to right, are Bruce Gibbs, Mick Shand and Ian 'Tuska' McNeil. Neither Gibbs or McNeil flew during the 'Channel Dash', but 'just couldn't resist getting in the shot'. (*Air Force Museum of New Zealand/Public Domain*)

Flight Lieutenant Gary Barnett, on the left, and Sergeant Stan Browne pictured after their successful escapes from France. Both flew on *Rodeo* 64 from Kenley on 31 May 1942. The RAF aircraft were attacked by thirty Fw 190s and both Barnett and Browne were shot down. They evaded capture and returned to the UK later in 1942. (*R.J. Taylor, via P.R. Arnold*)

There were all the facilities of a permanent RAF station again, and our dispersal was opposite to that of 452 Squadron RAAF, along with 602 (City of Glasgow) Squadron, whose CO at the time was Squadron Leader Alan Deere, another New Zealander. We also had the option of local pubs and we could get into Croydon in the evening for entertainment. London was also only a short run by taxi or train if time allowed.

During 485's first month at RAF Kenley Squadron Leader Knight was awarded the Distinguished Flying Cross, but he also relinquished command to Squadron Leader 'Hawkeye' Wells. It was also whilst 485 was at RAF Kenley that it took part in an operation that came to be known as the 'Channel Dash'.

The German pocket battleships Gneisenau, Prinz Eugen *and* Scharnhorst *were in Brest. The German plan was that they would break out of Brest and charge up the English Channel*

Two of Joe's groundcrew colleagues, Leading Aircraftman Jackson and Corporal Cross, pose for the camera in front of Flight Lieutenant Reginald William Baker's Spitfire, 'OU-B', at RAF Kenley. (*Air Force Museum of New Zealand/Public Domain*)

to the relative safety of home ports using the cover of bad weather. They sailed under the cover of darkness on 11 February.

The following day 485 was scrambled as part of the Allies' efforts to challenge the German break-out. In the subsequent combats with covering German fighters, Crawford-Compton and Reg Grant claimed two enemy aircraft destroyed. Dave Clouston and Harvey Sweetman made a joint claim for another, while Flight Lieutenant Francis claimed a Fw 190 and Sergeant Rae probably destroyed a Bf109. The New Zealanders' exploits made the newspapers and brought 485 into the limelight.

One of 485 Squadron's Spitfires that would not be returning to undergo the attention of Joe and his colleagues. This is W3579, coded 'OU-O' and named *Southland II*, force-landed in shallow water on a French beach on 31 October 1941. The pilot at the time was Wing Commander E.N. Ryder. (*Air Force Museum of New Zealand/Public Domain*)

Flight Lieutenant Edward Preston 'Hawkeye' Wells DFC & Bar, in the cockpit of a 485 Squadron Spitfire named *Waikato*. (*Air Force Museum of New Zealand/Public Domain*)

The groundcrew having finished their preparations, Flying Officer Johnny Pattison is pictured in the cockpit of his 485 (NZ) Squadron Spitfire, BM239 coded 'OU-N'. (*Air Force Museum of New Zealand/Public Domain*)

My promotion to corporal came through at Kenley. This meant that I was now responsible to the senior NCO for the tradesmen and discipline on 'A' Flight. I also found myself employed on any of the 'A' Flight aircraft.

We stayed at Kenley for nearly seven months. I remember that when we were off duty, visits took place to Croydon ice rink and the Greyhound pub. Also, there was a wonderful Christmas dance held at the hotel at the bottom of Whyteleafe Hill. Our CO, Reg Grant, threw out some of the RAF Police when they tried to curtail some of our more enthusiastic revellers.

It was not all fun, as I have other memories of cold, frosty nights spent at dispersal struggling with large nylon material covers for the aircraft to protect them from the frost and ice. The worst piece of this protective gear was the trouble in fitting the engine

Joe with fellow members of 485 (NZ) Squadron's groundcrew at RAF Kenley. This picture was taken shortly after Joe's promotion to the rank of Corporal. (*Mark Hillier Collection*)

Not a normal role for a member of 485 Squadron's groundcrew – here an unidentified Corporal is acting as the squadron's barber outside a dispersal hut at RAF Kenley. (*Air Force Museum of New Zealand/Public Domain*)

One of 485 Squadron's pilots, Evan Dall Mackie, flanked by two members of the squadron's groundcrew at RAF Kenley in 1942. Note the nose art, in the form a rose symbol, which can be seen below the Spitfire's windscreen. It was whilst flying from Kenley that Mackie, who went on to become a Wing Commander with the DSO, DFC and Bar, achieved his first victory. (*Air Force Museum of New Zealand/Public Domain*)

One of 485 (NZ) Squadron's Spitfire, W3774, pictured at RAF Kenley in 1942 with groundcrew about to start work on battle damage that can be seen just below the cockpit windscreen. This aircraft was flown by Flight Lieutenant W.V. Crawford-Compton. Note the name *Auckland 1 'Waiuku'* and the caricature of Hitler in a frying pan over a burning swastika. (*Air Force Museum of New Zealand/Public Domain*)

Three groundcrew servicing a 485 (NZ) Squadron Spitfire at RAF Kenley in 1942. They are, left to right, Corporal Muir, Corporal Ernie Bongard, and Leading Aircraftman Hooper. (*Air Force Museum of New Zealand/Public Domain*)

Another view of Joe's colleagues, Corporal Muir, Corporal Ernie Bongard, and Leading Aircraftman Hooper, at work on a 485 Squadron Spitfire at Kenley in 1942. (*Air Force Museum of New Zealand/Public Domain*)

Some of 485 (NZ) Squadron's armourers loading ammunition into the wing of a Spitfire. On the wing is Leading Aircraftman A.W. Martin, whilst below him are Leading Aircraftman Ernie Bongard (on the left) and Aircraftman 1st Class J.B. Neville. (*Air Force Museum of New Zealand/Public Domain*)

With the groundcrew having almost certainly prepared it for its next sortie, one of 485 Squadron's pilots, possibly Flight Lieutenant R.W. Baker, is pictured standing beside Spitfire 'OU-F' at RAF Station Kenley. (*Air Force Museum of New Zealand/Public Domain*)

An informal photograph of a group of 485's pilots relaxing outside a dispersal hut at RAF Station Kenley in 1942. Invariably, at moments like this the groundcrew were hard at work preparing the Spitfires for their next sortie. (*Air Force Museum of New Zealand/Public Domain*)

Sergeant Doug Brown in the cockpit of his Mk V Spitfire who was posted to 485 at Kenley on 5 December 1941. (*Hamish Brown*)

Two pilots and three groundcrew of 485 Squadron standing in front of a Spitfire in 1942. They are, left to right: Flight Sergeant Morris (in charge of maintenance); Flight Lieutenant Pattison; Flight Sergeant Wormwall ('B' Flight); Flight Lieutenant Baker; Flight Sergeant Gray ('A' Flight). (*Air Force Museum of New Zealand/Public Domain*)

covers. These contained a metal box for the oil heater and the thick quilting completely enveloped the engine ending in this box affair hanging down. The metal box contained a catalytic heater which took ages to light and was usually out when we uncovered the aircraft in the morning. The whole lot had to then be folded neatly and hung in a hut at dispersal which also housed all the anti-gas protection gear for the groundcrew.

The hut was heated by oil stoves to prevent the gas capes sticking together, and one day old 'Nobby' Hall, a rigger whose job included keeping the stoves topped up with fuel, was observed running like a hare towards the flight sergeant's office and shouting 'FIRE'. He had a terrible stutter and by the time he had convinced the flight sergeant that the gas hut was on fire the whole lot, contents and building, were just a pile of ash!

Flying Officer R.W. Baker examines the damage to the rudder and elevators of his 485 (NZ) Squadron Spitfire circa 1941 or 1942 – the repairs of which would soon require the attention of Joe and his colleagues. (*Air Force Museum of New Zealand/Public Domain*)

Eight frames of gun camera film showing a Fw 190 being shot down by 485's Flight Sergeant Robson in May 1942. One frame shows German fighter's canopy coming off, while another couple show the pilot baling out. Despite this, the original caption states that this was only recorded as a 'probable'. (*Air Force Museum of New Zealand/Public Domain*)

Pilots and groundcrew of 485 (NZ) Squadron photographed at Kings Cliffe. (*R.J. Taylor, via P.R. Arnold*)

Some of 485 (NZ) Squadron's pilots pictured at Kings Cliffe in 1942. On the far right is Flight Sergeant Lesley 'Chalky' White, who was one of the squadron's larger than life characters. As Joe once said, he had, 'Hands as large as shovels'. He survived the war and returned to New Zealand to become a sheep farmer. Fifth from left is Reg Grant, who had recently taken over as the squadron boss. Though the squadron had moved to Kings Cliffe for a rest, it continued to suffer losses. These included Flight Sergeant M.N. Langlands, who was posted missing following a sortie attacking trains in the area of the Franco-Belgian border on 2 August 1942. A further casualty occurred the day after, when Flight Sergeant R. Vessey went missing in the same circumstances. (*R.J. Taylor, via P.R. Arnold*)

We headed north again at the beginning of July 1942, this time to the Peterborough area. Our destination was a small airfield designated WB2. Though officially called Wansford, as the nearest village was Kings Cliffe, we always referred to it as Kings Cliffe. It really was a temporary affair and was, I think, along with Colley Weston just a satellite for the nearby permanent RAF camp at Wittering. The facilities were sparse, the barracks – Nissen huts – were certainly spartan, but being a Corporal I was lucky, I had a small bunk at one end of the hut to myself. Luxury!

The squadron generally undertook aerodrome defence and patrols, with the occasional free-lance fighter sortie over Belgium and Holland to keep sharp. These latter sorties, however, came at a high cost, with the squadron losing three pilots in the space of two weeks.

We were very busy at Kings Cliffe, the pilots flying off on ops such as the low-flying *Rangers* and *Rhubarbs*. Apparently very necessary, and something to do with shooting up anything in France with a black cross that moved.

What off duty time we got was either spent in the NAAFI or at the two pubs in Wansford, a short walk from the camp. The Mermaid Inn was for the rough amongst us, and the Haycock Hotel for the elite. I frequented the Mermaid.

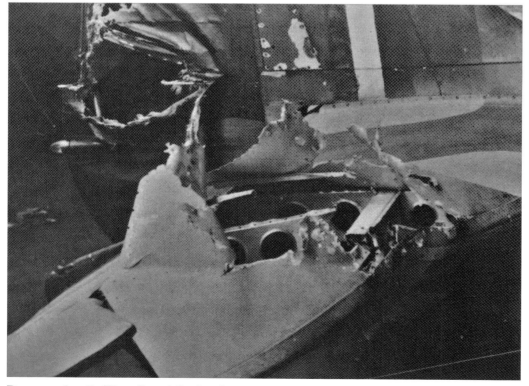

Damage to the tail of Doug Brown's Spitfire after a sortie out of Kings Cliffe attacking trains on the Continent. (*Hamish Brown*)

Just one of the many obstacles and challenges that the groundcrew of 485 (NZ) Squadron were faced with during their time at RAF Kings Cliffe (which Joe also referred to as Wansford) – a tractor and hay bailer at work around the dispersal area. Note Spitfire 'OU-K' behind. (*Air Force Museum of New Zealand/Public Domain*)

Groundcrew and other personnel pushing 485's Spitfire 'OU-S' backwards in a photograph believed to have been taken at RAF Station King's Cliffe. (*Air Force Museum of New Zealand/Public Domain*)

The pub used by quite a few of the pilots and groundcrew was reached by a walk across the airfield. It meant groping your way back in the dark at closing time and dodging parked Spitfires. Once or twice small incidents occurred that resulted in minor damage to the aircraft. Our CO decided to put on an aircraft guard from dusk till dawn, two men at a time armed with a Thompson submachine-gun.

I was on guard with a friend one night when one of our favourite pilots, Les 'Chalky' White, and his closest friend, Tommy Tucker, were returning from the pub across the airfield with a group of men. They were in good voice and staggering a bit when I challenged them to 'Halt and be recognised'. I already knew who it was, but I was on guard and rules are rules.

There was a lot of 'shushing' and whispering before the huge bulk of Chalky loomed up in front of me, at which point he said, 'What o mate, what's that you got there?' He was of course referring to the Tommy Gun, and when he demanded 'Give us a look' you didn't refuse a bloke of Chalky's size.

He took the gun and pointing it skywards loosed off the entire drum of ammo. Needless to say all Hell broke loose. There were blokes running everywhere, but it was soon sorted out and hushed up.

Chalky was a hell of a bloke. He was not afraid of much, that for sure. His Spitfire was shot down over Occupied France in August 1943 and he was captured by the Germans.

Flying Officer H.S. Tucker, on the left, congratulates Pilot Officer 'Chalky' White upon the latter's safe return to 485 (NZ) Squadron after being shot down and evading capture. (*Air Force Museum of New Zealand/Public Domain*)

A success for the pilots and groundcrew of 485 (NZ) Squadron. A crowd has gathered around the still burning wreckage of a Dornier Do 217E-4 Wnr.1225 (U5 + AD) that was shot down by Flying Officer Lindsay Black on 3 August 1942. The aircraft crashed near Cranford, a small village on the outskirts of Kettering, killing all four crew members. (*Air Force Museum of New Zealand/Public Domain*)

Within forty-five minutes he had knocked out his guard and escaped. He wrote a book about his experiences, but when he got back to the squadron in October 1943, he told us all about his escapades. He had done plenty of walking, but he was also brazen enough to catch trains and was helped by French people, although during his attempt he was very nearly given away on one occasion.

He successfully made his way south to the Pyrenees. When he made it to Spain he headed for the British Consulate in Barcelona, but he was locked up as a suspected spy before he got there.

When Chalky got back to the UK, they were not going to let him fly with 485 again as it was said that he knew too much about the French Resistance and its helpers, which he might give away should he be shot down again and interrogated. Chalky was having none of it and he soon returned to the fold.

As a corporal I used to have to do Corporal of the Guard in the main area of the camp. This involved staying in the guardroom and organising the roster for those chaps on guard that night. One of the duties was to issue leave and forty-eight-hour passes from the guardroom before the full time RAF Police started at 8 a.m. When chaps were going far afield on leave – men such as Archie Jackson, the electrician to Oban, or some chaps to Cornwall, Wales or Ireland – they got their passes from me as soon as the full-time chaps packed up for the evening. These extra few hours meant quite a lot when twenty-four hours' travelling took a big chunk out of your seven day leave pass.

We had a detachment at RAF West Malling in Kent as part of the aerial cover for the Dieppe Raid in August 1942. We had a great time. The Spitfires were parked amongst the plum trees; needless to say we soon got sick of the sight of plums.

We were back at Kings Cliffe within a week. There were further detachments to Ireland, to an airfield called Kirkistown, and one to Egglington up north, but I didn't go to either.

I did one small detachment, one man of each trade, to a place called Docking in north Norfolk near the Wash. It was just a small landing strip with a few huts in case any of our aircraft were diverted or had to land before reaching base due to enemy action or mechanical trouble. We were to do whatever we could to get them flyable back to Kings Cliffe.

Only one Spitfire came, and that was at my request. The CO of the place, a flight lieutenant, tried to include me and my small party on the duty rosters, guard, fire picket etc., and he took our only means of transport off us. We had just two bicycles to get us to and from the field to the hut we lived in. A quick phone call to the squadron CO and he was there within the hour to sort things out. The officer never knew what hit him!

We didn't stay long at Docking and returned to Kings Cliffe to find everyone preparing for our next move. This, it turned out, was to be Westhampnett near Chichester in West Sussex.

We headed south to this satellite of RAF Tangmere in January 1943 and the squadron was soon operational within hours of arriving. We lived in huts a fair distance from the dispersal, but all facilities and food were good and there was plenty to do in Chichester any time we got off. I remember though that we would have to go to nearby RAF Tangmere for supplies if any of the our aircraft needed major work. We had some small blister hangars and one T2 hangar, but we could have three squadrons on the airfield at any one time, with the result that space was often at a premium.

RAF Westhampnett in 11 Group, was established on land belonging to Frederick Charles Gordon Lennox, Duke of Richmond and Gordon. An area of flat land near Goodwood was requisitioned by the Air Ministry, not with the idea of creating a fully operational airfield but an emergency landing ground. At this stage it was just literally a field with no purpose-built facilities.

It changed its status just prior to the Battle of Britain when it was upgraded to a satellite airfield of nearby RAF Tangmere. This brought some basic facilities, including a watch office, but it was essentially still just a grass field with a windsock. During the Battle of Britain, 145 Squadron under the command of Squadron Leader John Peel was the first unit to arrive with Hurricanes. The groundcrew were billeted in cow sheds, dog kennels and also at the racecourse, as well as tented accommodation.

In the winter of 1940/1941 the airfield was badly waterlogged, and a decision was made to put in a perimeter track and start erecting some blister hangars so that maintenance did not have to be carried out in the open. Even when 610 (County of Chester) Squadron moved in during the latter part of 1940, aircraft were still being taken through gaps in the hedges to an adjacent barn to be maintained. Most famously Douglas Bader flew his last operational trip from RAF Westhampnett in August 1941.

No.485 (NZ) Squadron was posted to RAF Westhampnett on 1 January 1943. Its six-month stay ended on 30 June 1943, when the squadron moved to RAF Biggin Hill. The Commanding Officer when the squadron moved in was Reginald Grant.

Three of of 485 (NZ) Squadron's pilots – Flight Lieutenant John Pattison, Squadron Leader Reginald Grant, the CO, and Flight Lieutenant Reginald Baker. Pattison had flown during the Battle of Britain with Nos. 92 and 266 squadrons. Reginald Grant was killed in 1944 after baling out of a Mustang too low. Baker, who had been the 'A' Flight commander, replaced Grant. Baker was killed whilst flying a de Havilland Mosquito on 22 February 1945, by when he been made CO of 487 (NZ) Squadron. (*Hamish Brown*)

One of 485 Squadron's Mk.V Spitfire, BM642 coded 'OU-A', pictured after a taxiing accident, possibly in early 1943 at Westhampnett. The aircraft was sent to Westlands for repair on 14 March 1943. (*Air Force Museum of New Zealand/Public Domain*)

Three of 485 Squadron's pilots photographed wearing flying gear near a dispersal hut at RAF Westhampnett in early 1943. Note the entrance to the air raid shelter on the left. Pictured from left to right are: Flying Officer Moorhead, Flight Lieutenant R.W. Baker, and Sergeant L.S.M. 'Chalky' White. Joe was particularly friendly with the latter. (*Air Force Museum of New Zealand/Public Domain*)

A further view of the upturned BM642 with a growing crowd of groundcrew, pilots and squadron personnel gathering round it. (*Air Force Museum of New Zealand/Public Domain*)

Another view of BM642, coded 'OU-A', after its taxiing accident. Note the groundcrew gathered on the left, no doubt pondering their next course of action. (*Air Force Museum of New Zealand/Public Domain*)

One of our pilots during our time at Westhampnett was Doug Brown. I have read some of his recollections in Hamish Brown's *Wine, Women and Song: A Spitfire Pilot's Story* (published by Fonthill Media in 2012): 'The Squadron was fully involved in operational duties and more often than not pilots were involved in two or more operations a day ... As this was a period when Fw 190s were making low level raids on South Coast towns, the Wing had a constant patrol operating from dawn to dusk. *Rhubarbs* were also carried out.

'I was deputy Flight Commander when, on dawn readiness on 11 April 1943, my number 2 and I were scrambled to cover the return of a damaged Stirling bomber. We located the aircraft, which was forced to make a landing in the sea a mile or so off Shoreham. All the crew except one had managed to clamber into the rubber dinghy.

'One crew member in his Mae West was drifting out to sea and I considered I could drop him my dinghy. I dropped the speed to 120mph, put down my flaps and with much difficulty managed to remove the dinghy from my parachute pack, which I was sitting on.

'I released the dinghy but forgot it had a lead attached and it caught the rudder area. Fortunately, the air pressure broke the cord as I had almost stalled due to the low speed. Regretfully it did not hit the target anyway, but a Walrus was soon on the scene and made the rescue.

'The Mermaid Hotel, about halfway from the aerodrome to Chichester, was well patronised by 485. Arthur King, the proprietor, was a very generous host, not only to 485 but all RAF squadrons. The squadron also utilised the services of the Kings Beach Hotel at Pagham. In the main we entertained our "friends "at Fishers Cottage.'

A party being held by 485 (NZ) Squadron during their time at RAF Westhampnett. Reg Grant is on the far left, while Doug Brown is in the centre. This party was one of many held in the property known as Fisher's Cottage, which was on the airfield's eastern boundary. One party held in this house got so out of hand there was a small fire in the upper bedrooms. (*Joe Roddis*)

Some of 485's groundcrew who Joe worked with pictured during a moment of downtime whilst at RAF Westhampnett. Some of the squadron's Spitfire Mk.Vs can be seen in the background. This photograph was taken on the south-east corner of the airfield, looking north towards the South Downs. (*Mark Hillier Collection*)

Doug Brown's Spitfire Mk.V carrying the artwork which he entitled 'Wine, Women and Song'. This was painted by one of Joe's friends, Vic Strange. A rigger, Vic can be seen in the centre of the three men on the wing. (*Hamish Brown*)

Doug Brown can be seen here on the right wearing his Mae West. Vic Strange is on the left. Joe remained in contact with a number of the groundcrew after the war, and, along with Vic Strange and Harry Mihalop, in later life was always a guest of Carolyn Grace at Spitfire ML407 supporters' events. (*Hamish Brown*)

One of Joe's snapshots taken at Westhampnett. A note written by Joe on the reverse indicates that the pilot was 'Bluey', the groundcrew 'Dev' and 'Knocker'. The latter was Ron 'Knocker' White, who was a fitter like Joe. Bluey was Sergeant Gordon H. Meagher, who was posted into 485 (NZ) Squadron in December 1942. Having left the unit in May 1943, he was eventually posted to 92 Squadron in Italy where he became a PoW. (*Mark Hillier Collection*)

Taken at Westhampnett in 1943, Joe can be seen in this photograph of some of 485 (NZ) Squadron's groundcrew gathered in front of Doug Brown's Mk.V – his head is just visible on the bottom right. Joe does not appear in many of his photographs; indeed, he used to tell me how much he hated having his picture taken. Vic Strange is in the cockpit. Note, once again, the distinctive artwork on Doug's Spitfire. (*Mark Hillier Collection*)

Some of 485 (NZ) Squadron's pilots in front of a Spitfire Mk.V at Westhampnett in January 1943. Among this group are the two Grant brothers, Ian and Reg, who are third and fourth from left respectively. Ian survived the Battle of Britain having flown with 151 Squadron, but was shot down during a sweep on 13 February 1943. Attacking a force of Fw 190s, 485's Spitfires were pounced on by a further twenty enemy fighters that joined the fray from out of the sun. Three Spitfires were shot down, one of which was Ian's – an event that was witnessed by his brother. Ian has no known grave and is remembered on the Runnymede Memorial. (*Mark Hillier Collection*)

On completion of its stay at Westhampnett, 485 then moved the short distance to RAF Merston, which was to the south of Chichester. This was only temporary, for it was followed shortly after by a relocation to RAF Biggin Hill. This move was to hold good fortune for Joe as there he met Betty Wood, a WAAF driver who was posted to the squadron.

At the start of July 1943, we moved to RAF Biggin Hill in Kent and exchanged our Mk.V Spitfires for the Mk IXb. A corporal fitter, Harry Mihalop from Ewell, and I were sent off on a course to the SU Carburettor factory at Stanmore to learn about the Bendix Stromberg

A portrait of Flying Officer Ian Allan Charles Grant, who was killed in action on 13 February 1942. (*Air Force Museum of New Zealand/Public Domain*)

Injection unit, as fitted to the Packard Merlin in some Spitfire Mk.IXs. I do remember on one occasion on one Spit we had fitted with a Packard, we had an engine problem which in our opinion was definitely a carb fault. We had both achieved a high pass mark on the course and we were happy and confident we could fix the issue, although it meant breaking the seals on the carbs which was, according to the manufacturer, strictly 'verboten'.

We were not deterred by this sort of law if it meant we could fix the Spitfire and get another flying, so out came the pliers, spanners and wire clippers and we set about fixing it away from the prying eyes of the engineering officer. Anyway the upshot was we fixed it and it flew.

Being a permanent station, Biggin Hill had all the facilities for our comfort and a good selection of local entertainment. We were always very busy, with lots of work, day after day to keep the aircraft flying. The pilots would know all the interesting details of where they flew and what they did, but it didn't interest us as long as they came back safely.

Sergeant Joe Roddis proudly sporting his new 'stripes' at Biggin Hill in 1943. (*Mark Hillier Collection*)

The New Zealand High Commissioner, W.J. Jordan (fifth from right), with one of 485's Spitfires at RAF Station Biggin Hill. (*Air Force Museum of New Zealand/Public Domain*)

It was at this time I was promoted to a sergeant engine fitter and discovered that the Sergeants' Mess was excellent. We hadn't been there long; I was up on the wing of a Spitfire when I noticed a small party of WAAFs walking down the perimeter track towards our dispersal. They were greeted by whistles and howls from the groundcrews as they headed towards our flight office. They were to be attached to the squadron for a short while. The group consisted of five airwomen and one corporal in charge, all being MT drivers.

They were at dispersal at all times – night and day – and there were no problems at all. Everybody behaved themselves, no swearing within earshot of 'em', and they did an excellent job driving, tractor towing 500-gallon fuel tankers for the Spitfires and so on. Some of the lads got together with them, going to dances in the off-duty hours.

I became very friendly with Corporal Betty Wood and we just seemed to be good for each other. She told me she was engaged to a Sergeant engine fitter stationed in the Middle East and that the rule of the day was 'no hanky panky'. This was perfectly understood and stuck rigidly too during the short time we were together. They had been together since school days and she was not looking for any other.

She wore the engagement ring all the time and I didn't need reminding. We would go up to London to the Hammersmith Palais, Covent Garden Opera House and other well-known dance halls whenever we were off duty together. We had fun, laughed at the same things and wanted to be together as often as we could.

Personnel of 485 (NZ) Squadron and other VIPs pictured at Biggin Hill on the occasion of the High Commissioner's visit in July 1943. Third from left, on the lefthand wing, is Flight Sergeant 'Chalky' White. Also in this group are Wing Commander A.G. 'Sailor' Malan (Station Commander) and Wing Commander A.C. Deere (Wing Commander Flying). (*Mark Hillier Collection*)

The New Zealand High Commissioner, W.J. Jordan, chatting with pilots of 485 (NZ) Squadron during a visit. Squadron Leader J.M. Checketts is on the far right. (*Air Force Museum of New Zealand/Public Domain*)

No.485 Squadron had taken over 611 Squadron's Spitfires when it had moved north for a rest. It was also whilst at Biggin Hill that Johnnie Checketts took over as the new CO. They also had some unexpected guests when pilots from the USAAF were posted in to gain tactical experience.

In 2011, I took Betty flying in a Super Cub from Goodwood and she told me her nickname whilst at Biggin Hill in 1943 had been 'Butch'. I was more than a little surprised, and enquired how she had come to acquire such a title. She explained that one of the American pilots posted to Biggin had offered her a flight in a Miles Magister and took her up with the sole intention of making her sick. When she

The well-known face of Wing Commander Alan Deere who was the Biggin Hill Wing Leader when Joe and 485 (NZ) Squadron arrived. Betty Wood, a WAAF driver who became Joe's dancing partner, frequently used to serve as the driver for Deere, as well as other well-known pilots like Sailor Malan and Johnnie Johnson. (*Mark Hillier Collection*)

got down she swiftly set about her unkind pilot, dealing him a kick in the shins. For this she giving the nickname 'Butch'.

Joe and the ground crew would have had the benefit of station workshops and decent hangars to help them carry out their jobs, as well as a good stock of spares.

August was not a good month for the unit with it suffering a number of losses, including Pilot Officer Les 'Chalky' White, who we have already encountered.

We left Biggin Hill around the middle of October 1943 and went to Hornchurch in Essex, another permanent RAF station, similar to Biggin Hill. Our WAAFs came with us. What I do remember about both airfields is that we had a shrapnel gathering brigade! Every morning after heavy raids on London, everyone would collect empty sandbags and clear the grass and runways of shrapnel, splinters and similar fragments. Our aircraft tyres wouldn't have lasted five minutes if we hadn't.

A 485 (NZ) Squadron photograph that was taken at RAF Hornchurch in October 1943. One of the squadron's new Spitfires Mk.IXs is serving as a backdrop. Identifiable pilots in this group include Flight Sergeant Herb Patterson, who is sitting on the propeller. Standing on the wing is Flying Officer A.B. Stead, who had flown on Malta with 249 Squadron and was later awarded a DFC. Sitting on the wing, left to the right, are: Sergeant John Yeatman, who went on to be commissioned and awarded the DFC; Roberts; Pilot Officer 'Chalky' White, who evaded capture after being shot down on 22 August 1943 and returned to the unit in October the same year, at which point he was commissioned, helping date this picture; Hugh Tucker; John 'Johnnie' Houlton, who was the pilot to claim the first victory over the D-Day beaches flying ML407; and Pilot Officer W.F. Bern, who was only with the squadron in October and November 1943. Meanwhile, in front row, left to right, are: Neville E. Frehner; unknown; Kenneth C. Lee; unknown; Flying Officer Lindsay Black, the flight commander of 'A' Flight, having taken over from Doug Brown and who was later awarded a DFC; Pilot Officer J.G. Dassent, the medical officer; unknown; Ian Strachen, who later commanded 65 Squadron, but was killed flying a Mustang in Norway; three more unknown men; and then, lastly, the Intelligence Officer, van Dyk. (*Mark Hillier Collection*)

Four of 485 Squadron's pilots in front of one of their Spitfires at RAF Station Hornchurch in November 1943. Left to right are: C.P. Ashworth (possibly visiting from 32 Squadron), J.A. Houlton, I.D.S. Strachan, J.F.P. Yeatman, and A.B. Stead. (*Air Force Museum of New Zealand/Public Domain*)

By this stage I had responsibility for both 'A' and 'B' flights. This was an exceptionally busy time on the flying side. Big wing formations, escorts and, I remember, visits from Al Deere who used to visit us there in a fancy Spitfire with all the rivet heads smoothed flush. The whole plane was polished like a cap badge. He said it definitely made the Spitfire go faster.

At Hornchurch the squadron was soon back in action and still mixing it with Fw 190s over the Continent. Then, in December, the squadron moved to Drem in Scotland for a well-earned rest.

Betty and I carried on as our friendship grew stronger, but this did not last much longer, as at this time it was decided to stand the aircrew down for a rest period of three months. It was a break from the operational flying, and the aircrew, plus three chosen groundcrew, moved up to Drem near North Berwick in Scotland. Some of our groundcrew were to remain behind, and they became 6485 Servicing Echelon, remaining at Hornchurch – along with Betty!

I was one of those heading to Drem. We were bussed off to Kings Cross station. We all helped load personal kit and squadron gear, including orderly room records, aboard the *Flying Scotsman*, on which we 'three' got a compartment to ourselves. It was a long journey north and the pilots did some merry making before we arrived at our destination towards the evening.

The short platform at North Berwick couldn't accommodate the full length of the train and it had to pull forwards to bring the squadron baggage car up to the station. Heads were poking out of every carriage to see what was causing the commotion. We struggled frantically to unload our gear. The CO was up the front arguing with the driver and eventually, after thirty minutes delay, the *Flying Scotsman* left for Edinburgh.

We were bussed up to Drem airfield by RNAS vehicles and it took some time to get used to the Fleet Air Arm types in the mess. The jargon too! 'Going ashore' instead of 'going off camp', saluting the quarter deck etc. Queer folk there with their navy blue uniforms and gold braid.

There was an experienced RAF groundcrew and a few worse for wear old Spitfires available at dispersal for the pilots to play with and they were kept here purely for the benefit of other Spitfire squadrons who might come for the same reason as we did. Very little flying was done, the pilots came down in odd ones and twos and flew around for an hour or so to keep their hand in.

I spent three weeks in hospital near Drem with suspected pneumonia after they found me lying on my bed in my bunk after not being seen for three days.

We were given the job of testing new pressurised flying suits. Our pilots would climb in to their Spitfires and then we filled the suits with hot water. The suits were an attempt to relieve pilots of the stresses and G forces whilst in tight turns and dives. We found them to be effective. However, our concern was heightened due to their bulkiness and weight. Thoughts of pilots having to make a quick escape from a burning aircraft did not endear them to us.

This concern was realised when Flying Officer John Dasent suffered engine trouble after flying too low and hit the sea on 22 December 1943. He managed to climb to 1,000 feet in an attempt to bale out, and was heard to curse the suit and its designers as he did so. Sadly he drowned. After his death we refused to continue tests.

By now it was February 1944 and it was time for 485 to move south again. Typically, Betty had been posted north to Inverness. We, meanwhile, were on our way back to Hornchurch. This time the transport arrangements were changed a bit. 'Chalky', now back with the squadron, was the proud owner of a car and Terry Kearins conjured up an old black Morris from somewhere.

In his newly acquired Singer Silent Six, 'Chalky' took a few pilots, while I travelled in the Morris with Terry. The remainder made the return trip by train. The two cars travelled in convoy and not long into the journey it started snowing heavily! With 'Chalky' taking short cuts through hedges and over fields (he would!) both cars eventually arrived at a small place called Wooler in Northumberland.

By now the snow was getting worse and we decided that a night stop there was the sensible thing to do. We found a small, inviting-looking hotel called Rose Cottage. We had a good night there, enjoying good food and the inevitable few beers. 'Chalky' got tangled up with a few brown jobs – Army personnel – when he saw them giving us funny looks.

A snapshot that belonged to one of 485 (NZ) Squadron's pilots, Max Collet. Max remained in touch with Joe after the war and the pair met several times at reunions. This photograph of 'B' Flight was taken at Hornchurch shortly after the squadron arrived from Scotland in early 1944. In the rear row is Flying Officer Wiliam Newenham, who had flown one tour on Whitleys and Wellingtons as an observer before becoming a fighter pilot, Pilot Officer Maurice 'Red' Mayston, Flight Sergeant R. Clark, Flying Offficer Allan Stead. who had flown from Malta, Pilot Officer Royce De Tourett, again a Malta veteran, Sergeant Frank Transom, and, lastly, Flight Lieutenant Ken Lee. In the front, from the left, are Flight Sergeant D. Clarke, Pilot Officer Athol Downer and Eddie Atkins. (*Max Collett*)

They appeared to resent the boisterous antics of the foreign 'Brylcream boys', so 'Chalky' took it upon himself to sort them out.

When it was time to set off the next morning we had to dig the cars out of the snow. Unfortunately, the big Singer refused to start. Again 'Chalky' took control, poured a lot of petrol into the air intake, so when it did finally burst into life the whole engine was enveloped in flames. 'Chalky' whipped off his new RAF officer's great coat, smothered the flames and we were on our way.

We parted company on the A1 south of Doncaster as I had persuaded Terry to pay a visit with me to my parents at my home in Sheffield. They were very surprised when I turned up – even more so when I introduced them to Terry, a New Zealand Spitfire pilot. My dad couldn't take his eyes off him. Most civilians had only heard or read about fighter pilots, and for my dad this was a definite must for discussion with his pals at work.

No.485 Squadron was now to become part of the 2nd Tactical Air Force, 2nd TAF, in preparation for D–Day and the invasion of France. Along with Nos. 222 and 349 squadrons, it was to form

135 Wing. Moves were now frequent as the unit set out to familiarise itself with being mobile, as would be the case once they were shipped over to France after the Allied landings.

We arrived back at the end of February 1944 and the groundcrew welcomed us back. It was not long before we were on the move again. This time for gunnery and bombing practice at Llanbedor in North Wales. We did a lot of flying and the pilots were ready for it after their rest. We had our own squadron Spitfires back again. Within two weeks we returned to Hornchurch, with one further small detachment, which I didn't go on, heading to Great Stampford.

Our next move was to one of our best remembered airfields – the Advanced Landing Ground, or ALG, at Selsey.

As preparations for D-Day continued, the number of airfields along the South Coast increased dramatically to accommodate the growing number of squadrons that were preparing for the day the Allies would launch their invasion fleet across the Channel. Operation Overlord *would require air support to succeed and once a foothold had been established it would be important for these squadrons to be able to operate from rough and ready airstrips.*

Both the air and groundcrew would need to be able to operate with minimum support and be asked to move at a moment's notice. Around Chichester the airspace was crowded with aircraft operating from the airfields at Tangmere, Selsey, Ford, Merston, Appuldram, Coolham, Funtington and Bognor.

Selsey ALG had been set up on what was a pre-war airfield dating back to the early 1930s, a grass strip that had been home to Moths and other light aircraft. It was frequented by RAF aircraft long before it was taken over and expanded for fulltime RAF use. Accommodation at Selsey was basic to say the least, not just for the groundcrew but the pilots as well. Almost everyone lived in the field under canvas come rain or shine.

By the beginning of April 1944 the whole squadron seemed to sense that for us our part in the war and the 2nd TAF had really started to come alive. The pilots were continually airborne. The weather was good, and I think we were all pleased to be back under canvas again. It was an easier life style in tents rather than in permanent accommodation. We were, after all, much closer to the aircraft. Just a few yards to walk and you were at your Spitfire, which was very convenient.

A Mk.IX, Spitfire ML407, better known today as the Grace Spitfire, joined the squadron at Selsey. Given the codes OU-V, it was almost immediately involved in all the action that was now taking place from Selsey. It was at Selsey that we had to apply invasion stripes to our aircraft. Over the years many people ask me about how we applied them, and did the aircraft look right? I tell them that we had black and white distemper and we applied it with yard brushes! We didn't have lots of time for masking up and painting nice straight lines, that was for sure. They all look too neat now on the Spitfires.

8.   Distemper.

        All Servicing Echelons and Wing Headquarters of
2nd T.A.F. and No. 85 Group should hold sixteen distemper brushes
per day squadron served.   Air Sea Rescue Squadrons should hold
one brush per I.E. aircraft.

        Equipment Sections of Stations and of 2nd T.A.F.
and No. 85 Group Wings should hold distemper ready for immediate
issue on the basis of 2½ gallons of night distemper and 3½ gallons
of white distemper for each day fighter type aircraft and 3½
gallons of night distemper and 5 gallons of white distemper for
each Walrus or Warwick Air Sea Rescue aircraft.

            Note: A proportion of the issue will be an oil
            based distemper which will require a longer period
            to dry, but must nevertheless be used wherever
            practicable.   Issue of the necessary distemper
            for all Units is being arranged.

One of three sections from 11 Group's Administration Instructions for Operation *Overlord*. This part contains information for the use and availability of distemper. (*Mark Hillier Collection*)

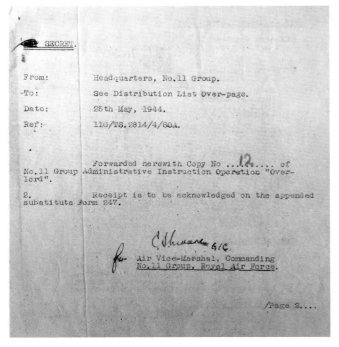

SECRET.

From: Headquarters, No.11 Group.

To: See Distribution List Over-page.

Date: 25th May, 1944.

Ref: 11G/TS.2814/4/SOA.

        Forwarded herewith Copy No ...12.... of
No.11 Group Administrative Instruction Operation "Overlord".

2.   Receipt is to be acknowledged on the appended
substitute Form 247.

                C.Steward GIC.
        for Air Vice-Marshal, Commanding
            No.11 Group, Royal Air Force.

                                /Page 2....

The covering page of copy No.12 of 11 Group's Administration Instructions for Operation *Overlord*. This shows the date of issue as 25 May 1944. (*Mark Hillier Collection*)

-2-

SECTOR.	GROUP.	SECTOR HQ.	WING HQ.	SQDN.	STATION.	TYPE OF AIRCRAFT.
TANGMERE	84	18 (F)	131 (Pole)	(302(P) (308 (P) (317 (P)	Chailey ALG. " "	Spit.IX.IF.IR. " " " " " "
"	"	"	133 (Pole)	(306 (P) (315 (P) (129	Coolham ALG. " "	Mustang III. " " " "
"	"	"	135	(222 (349 (Belge) (485 (RNZAF)	Selsey ALG. " "	Spit.IX.IF. " " " "
"	TAF		34	-	Northolt.	
"	"		"	(16 (140 (69	" " "	Spit.XI.PR. Spit.XI.PR. Mos.XI.XVI.PR. Wellington. XIII.
"	85	-	141	(264 (322(Dutch)	Hartford Bridge. "	Mos. XIII. Spit.XIV.
"	"	-	142	-	Horne ALG.	
"	11	-	"	(303(P) (130 (402(RCAF)	Horne ALG. " "	Spit.V.IF.IR. " " " " " "

Our third and final section from 11 Group's Administration Instructions for Operation *Overlord*. This order of battle contains 485 (NZ) Squadron at Selsey. (*Mark Hillier Collection*)

Though poor quality, this is an air-to-air view of Spitfire ML407 which, coded 'OU-V', was delivered to 485 (NZ) Squadron at Selsey. It was operational on D-Day. This picture was actually taken on 27 August 1944, the pilot being Johnnie Houlton. Lovingly restored post-war by Nick Grace, who was to tragically be killed in a car accident, ML407 has continued to be operated by the Grace family and its supporters. Joe was very proud of his association with both ML407 and the Grace family. (*Kearins Eqs, via the Peter Arnold Collection*)

Records show that ML407 was delivered to the squadron on 30 April 1944. Once at Selsey, it was allocated to Flying Officer John 'Johnnie' Houlton, who was to undertake the most operational sorties in this particular Spitfire. The first operation ML407 took part in occurred a week later, although on this occasion she was flown by Flight Lieutenant Keith Macdonald. He formed part of the escort for eight other 485 (NZ) Squadron Spitfires which were carrying 500lb bombs to attack a target in the Pas de Calais.

ML407 dropped its first bomb on 20 May, when the squadron was tasked with attacking a V1 launch site that was under construction at Éclimeux. This was a role that the squadron was to become very familiar with throughout May 1944.

Time off was unheard-of while we were at Selsey, except for the odd spot of leave and the occasional twenty-four or forty-eight-hour pass. I thought I would never see Betty again following her transfer to Inverness, but her home was in Worthing, not too far from Selsey.

One day whilst on leave from Scotland she visited Selsey to see me. I was away for the day on some job or other and didn't get to see her, but she did contact me by letter asking if I could possibly meet her at Worthing. I agreed. Things were arranged and I swung a twenty-four hour pass. She met me at the station in Worthing and told me that her fiancé had arrived back in the UK and would be with her in a few days.

The situation was emotional, but I had given her my word. I was not about to spoil it all now. She wanted to go to a tea dance in Worthing town hall. We had just one dance, our favourite, a slow foxtrot. When I came to leave her at Worthing station on my return to Selsey, she became very emotional and left in tears. I thought I would never see her again.

We had soon settled into a good routine at Selsey. Food was good, flying took place all day, every day, and we'd made the tents comfortable. I used to take the pilots up to RAF Tangmere once a week to get a bath and do laundry etc. It was a good excuse for me to drive the Commanding Officers' car.

Veterans in front of ML407. Joe is standing second from the left. On his right is Warrant Officer Peter Hale, a Spitfire pilot with 41 Squadron. On the other side of Joe are Vic Strange and Harry Mihalop, who had both been groundcrew on 485 (NZ) Squadron. (*Mark Hillier Collection*)

This picture of some of 485 (NZ) Squadron's groundcrew was taken by Joe – he had managed to avoid another photograph! On the left is Vic Strange; the others are sadly not annotated on the rear. It is believed to have been taken at Selsey in 1944. (*Mark Hillier Collection*)

One of 485's pilots, Flying Officer Frank Transom, standing second from the left, pictured with his groundcrew in front of his Spitfire at RAF Selsey in June 1944. (*Air Force Museum of New Zealand/Public Domain*)

A photograph that shows the conditions that Joe and his 485 Squadron colleagues encountered at RAF Selsey. Left to right are: J.A. Houlton, F. Transom, R.H. De Tourret, and A.J. Downer. (*Air Force Museum of New Zealand/Public Domain*)

Often on the way back we would head into Chichester for a few drinks. But on one occasion this nearly caused me to crash into a pub on the way back to camp. The car was overloaded and as I hit a 90-degree bend in the road, I nearly lost the backend. Somehow I managed to recover it, but I do have a little chuckle every time I drive past that pub on my way home to Selsey.

One incident I do remember was that we were doing a lot of dive-bombing in the period leading up to D-Day. We would bomb our Spitfires up with 500lb bombs and off they would go to soften up targets. The bomb was released from the aircraft by a battery-operated solenoid and these were not immune to failure. The button for release was mounted on the stick.

The standing orders were that if a pilot had a hang up, they were to try and shake it loose. Should that fail, or it was not possible for any reason, they should point the bloody thing out to sea and get out on the parachute, not to bring it home with them. Despite these instructions, on one occasion a pilot came back to the airfield with a hang up and tried to wheel it on gently. The bomb, however, choose that moment to fall away and merrily bounced off the underside of the aircraft. We could all see it happening in what felt like slow motion – needless to say we all ran like hell, not waiting to see where this damn thing ended up.

The second incident, which quite a few of us witnessed, was when a USAAF Thunderbolt appeared overhead and slightly to the left of the airfield perimeter flying at about 500 feet. It appeared to be flying very slowly and making weird engine noises as if it was running out of fuel.

As we watched, the pilot stepped out of the cockpit on to the mainplane, waited a short time, then jumped! He just went straight down; his chute didn't fully open and he hit the deck. The Thunderbolt went in to a flat spin down and exploded on impact. There was not a lot left of the pilot or aircraft. The poor soul had probably been at the end of a long daylight bomber escort and run out of fuel over Selsey.

We were really busy now, beach-head patrols and shooting up everything and anything German that might menace the landing troops and equipment. We crowded round the pilots as they returned from ops to get the latest 'gen' on how things were going.

Soon, though, the day that we had been training for was upon us. Monday, 5 June had been a normal working day, with operations continuing from dawn to dusk. But we all sensed that something was in the air – a feeling exacerbated by the increased coming and going by intelligence personnel and top brass.

Towards the end of the day, the reason became obvious. The sky filled with big four-engine jobs all towing huge gliders. There were all sorts – Dakotas, Stirlings, Lancasters and so on, all heading out over the Channel. It had started: D-Day. It just went on and on as we stood watching and wondering, how are those troops feeling?

One Stirling passed over with the glider tow rope looped around its tail causing them both to fly at a very awkward angle! We later learned that the airborne troops in the glider had elected to jump once over water. They all perished.

Johnnie Houlton was one of our pilots who got the first claim on D-Day itself. One of our pilots actually shot down a Spitfire that kept pestering him, despite all his attempts to convince the other pilot he was not the enemy. It later turned out to have been a Seafire, the Navy's version of the Spitfire, that was being flown by a 'novice' pilot.

One sad episode which happened during this hectic period during and after D-Day involved a very good and well-liked airframe fitter, Sergeant Frank Henry Reeve. But it should have been me, as I returned from a day away to find that he had been killed doing the job I would normally have done. It was a sad loss, as Frank was a married man with children, as well as an athlete of some note.

As was the normal procedure after any engine work that required a ground test, three men would sit on a Spitfire's tail to hold it down as the fitter doing the run up opened up to full throttle. My place as engine sergeant would be to oversee the safety of the run, for which I would stand by the port wing tip in full view of the cockpit.

On one occasion on 13 August 1944, at full throttle a Spitfire's engine seemed to exceed maximum RPM and the aircraft tipped over on to its nose. Its propellor shattered and pieces flew all over the place. One sadly took off the side of Frank's head. Vic Strange saw the incident and said there was nothing that could be done to save him.

Another witness that day was Johnnie Houlton, who wrote the following in his book *Spitfire Strikes* (which was published by John Murray in 1985):

'The engine involuntarily went from ticking over to 3000 rpm and maximum power in one brief, roaring surge. The machine whipped nose-down over the chocks and the tail flicked high in the air, as I could see the fitter wrenching at the throttle in the cockpit. A great deluge of earth and debris exploded upwards as the four wooden propeller blades smashed into splinters against the ground, and the two airmen on the tail were catapulted high in the air, like helpless, tumbling puppets.

'The stubs of the propeller blades clawed the Spitfire round to the left through an arc of ninety degrees, as the left chock held firm, but the right wheel pushed its chock clear. A body hurtled through the air out of the maelstrom, then the engine stopped dead, leaving a vibrating, shocking silence.

'I ran to the crumpled body, but Frank Reeves had died instantly; then I checked one of the airmen thrown from the tail, who had some broken ribs.'

All the correct safety precautions had been adhered to for the test, but we never really found out the cause of the tragedy. My own theory was that after the boost adjustment, a thing we were continually doing those days, a throttle linkage check was always carried out. Particular attention was applied to the small stainless-steel retaining clip where the rods were joined at the cross shaft. If this clip worked loose, the engine was uncontrollable and would just fly up to max throttle or even beyond. We never did find out what the Technical Board of Enquiry came up with – but that would not have helped Frank.

A member of 485's groundcrew in the cockpit of Spitfire ML377, which was coded 'OU-Y', at Selsey in 1944. Its normal pilot was Terry Kearins, who allowed Joe to paint the name of his girlfriend Mary, who would later become his wife, on the side of the fuel tank. Terry was shot down in July 1943, but managed to evade capture and returned to 485 whilst it was at Drem. (*Mark Hillier Collection*)

The badly damaged tail of Spitfire Mk.IX ML400, coded OU-N, which was being flown by Pilot Officer Herbert Patterson when it was hit by flak during a *Ranger* sortie over the Netherlands in May 1944. The squadron was operating from Selsey at the time. Patterson managed to nurse the aircraft back to Bradwell Bay, where this picture was taken. He signed this photograph and gave it to Joe. (*Mark Hillier Collection*)

Being part of 2nd TAF meant being mobile and living under canvas. This picture illustrates just how basic the squadron's accommodation was at this point. 'Chalky' White is the individual sat in the bath, while Frank Transom is washing his hair on the right. (*Max Collett*)

One of 485's groundcrew poses by a tent at Selsey just before D-Day. Joe lived not far from the airfield in later life and when I dropped him home from a signing or day out he would always show me the spot just behind the hedge where he remembered their camp was. Next door was a little farm cottage, which he noted the pilots soon commandeered! (*Mac Collett*)

Chapter 6

A Flying Bomb at Funtington

Life No.5

We were now officially 485 (NZ) Squadron, 84 Fighter Group, 135 Wing, 2nd Tactical Air Force. Mobility exercises were coming thick and fast in preparation for when our turn came to go to Normandy. At very short notice we'd pack up everything into the fleet of vehicles we now operated ourselves instead of having to rely on a separate MT section. All the groundcrew now found themselves also acting as drivers of the squadron's vehicles, no matter whether it was the 3-ton Chevys, low-loaders, Commer vans, de-icer units, radio trucks or Jeeps. I drove the CO's Fordson V8 Shooting Brake. We made quite a convoy when we were on the move.

On one occasion in July we carried out a three-day mobility exercise from Selsey to Coolham. Then from the latter we headed across to Funtington. This involved all three of the squadrons in the Wing – Nos. 222, 349 and 485 squadrons.

We liked Funtington. The weather was great, and our tents were pitched amongst the trees at dispersal with the aircraft close by. Any time off was spent doing chores, laundry, letter writing etc. While we were at Funtington we had a visit from the New Zealand High Commissioner, who handed out 'Ciggys' and NZ fruit cake – which was lovely.

One of the wireless chaps by the name of Sprowson had set himself the task of sorting out where the livelier action was at! Fortnightly, some of us would go to a dance he had sniffed out at a nearby place called Emsworth. It was a favourite place of some of the ATS girls from Havant and I met my wife there who was in the ATS at that time.

We were very busy at Funtington, working from dawn to dusk. We always seemed to be changing the additional fuel tanks. We called them drop tanks and they came in various shapes and sizes. Plywood and fabric 'slipper' tanks, 30- and 45-gallon size. There were also 90-gallon circular shaped metal ones. We had been using drop tanks for a long time now, but never with the same intensity as we were doing at Funtington.

It was about now that the V1 flying bombs, or Doodlebugs, started making their presence felt. There seemed to be a constant stream passing daily overhead our airfield.

A few of the lads had elected to pitch their tent on the opposite side of the dispersal to us, in front of a huge collection of drop tanks. The lads, Harry Mihalop, Tom Prickett, Archie Jackson, 'Ginger' Archer, and Tony Moore, were all quietly enjoying the usual cuppa during a break when a V1 appeared overhead.

It was at this point that its engine suddenly stopped! In total silence the Doodlebug dived towards the pile of drop tanks where it then impacted and exploded with an ear-splitting crash. Earth, drop tanks and debris were thrown everywhere.

Two pilots, Pilot Officer M.C. Mayston and Flying Officer R.H. De Tourret, pictured walking away from their aircraft at RAF Funtington in late July or early August 1944. The two members of groundcrew watching on the left are Joe's colleagues Flight Sergeant Bongard and Sergeant Parker. (*Air Force Museum of New Zealand/Public Domain*)

Everyone watching set off at a run towards the lone tent, expecting to find the occupants crushed. We were met halfway by them galloping towards us completely unscathed. The drop tanks had absorbed the blast and protected them from death and injury.

By now the pilots were making regular landings on makeshift airfields in Normandy, on runways constructed off Pierced Steel Planking, or PSP, so one of the most important tasks we were carrying out was checking the Spitfires' tyres when they returned in case they had been damaged by these improvised runways. One good thing was that the pilots often brought back with them bottles of Vichy water or Calvados.

We moved back to Selsey again in August 1944, though we were all itching to get over the Channel! Rumours were flying around as to when and where we would go, and towards the end of the month things started to become pretty certain. We had been issued with some 'funny money', as used by the troops over there, and we were just waiting for Caen to fall to enable the First Canadian Army to move north, at which point we'd be off to Normandy.

Eventually after heavy fighting, shelling and bombing, they managed to get the fanatical SS troops out and the army moved across the only river bridge into Caen for their continuing push north. I had planned to meet my future wife, Mary, on her birthday, which was 26

Above: A gang of 485's groundcrew manoeuvring the CO's Spitfire by hand at Funtington ALG. The fact it was his is denoted by the pennant on the port side. Joe is the one with no shirt pushing on the propeller. This was the mount of Squadron Leader Johnnie Niven, who was the only CO not to be a New Zealander. The Spitfire is NH321, which was one of the aircraft destroyed on the ground during *Bodenplatte*. The aircraft behind is ML354, coded 'OU-P', which was damaged whilst attacking trains on 24 August 1944. On that occassion it was being flown by Flight Lieutenant Owen L. Hardy. (*Mark Hillier Collection*)

Left: 'The Boss', Squadron Leader Johnnie Niven, in front of his Spitfire, Mk.IX NH321. (*Mark Hillier Collection*)

A group of Douglas C-47 Dakotas of the 439th Troop Carrier Group pictured at an airfield in England on 7 June 1944. Joe took off from RAF Tangmere, bound for France as part of 485 (NZ) Squadron's advance party, on 26 August. (*Historic Military Press*)

A 485 (NZ) Squadron group photograph taken at Funtington ALG in 1944. (*Max Collett*)

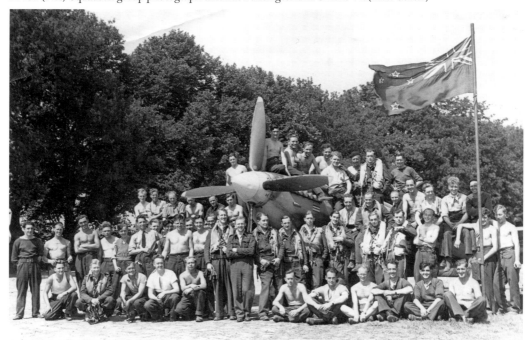

August, but I was in the advance party heading for RAF Tangmere and the Dakotas that were standing by waiting to take us to Caen-Carpiquet airfield.

I made the following entry in my diary that day: 'Took off in Dakota aircraft from RAF T [Tangmere] at 11:50 hours for France. Landed after uneventful trip at 13:40 hrs on Carpiquet Airfield (Caen). Pitched tents on quite good site and commenced opps [operations]. Place in absolute ruins after visit by bomber boys, also naval shelling. Hun graves everywhere and one Sherman tank knocked out by an anti-tank shell. Crew all buried around the tank. One building only in use. German officers mess used by Canadians and our wing for a canteen and ENSA Concert party. Also saw a film "his butlers sister". [*His Butler's Sister* is a 1943 American romantic comedy film directed by Frank Borzage and starring Deanna Durbin.]

The remainder of the lads came over by boat with all the trucks and the rest of the equipment, going ashore through one of the Mulberry harbours to finally reach the airfield on 31 August.

Chapter 7

Werewolves!

Life No.4

No sooner has we arrived in Normandy than we pitched our tents and set about getting ourselves sorted out as we waited for the Spitfires to arrive. I was straight into the routine again and it was a bit hectic. We, the groundcrew, were at half-strength until the rear party arrived by boat, but somehow we coped.

The few locals we encountered were openly hostile as they had suffered somewhat during the invasion period. Also, their previously organised lives under occupation had somewhat been disturbed.

We were also undoubtedly in a war zone. We could not show any lights at all after dark. There were booby traps everywhere, snipers were a very real risk and some very unsavoury characters calling themselves Werewolves were intent on doing us harm.

In the late summer and early autumn of 1944, Heinrich Himmler initiated Operation Werwolf, *the plan being to establish an elite unit of volunteer personnel to operate secretly behind the Allies' lines. In some cases, the intention was for these men to wear Allied uniforms and use the enemy's weapons.*

Rumours of a secret Nazi guerrilla organization began to surface soon after the invasion of Normandy – hence Joe's apprehension. As he also pointed out, booby traps were rife in and around the invasion area. One example of these involved the Germans stretching thin steel cables across roads at head height, so that when a jeep or motorbike came roaring down the road, its driver and passengers might be decapitated. It is known that they also connected hand grenades to the dog tags of dead soldiers, so that anyone who tried to remove the identity discs was blown up.

Whilst at Carpiquet [officially known as airfield B17] I'd had a trip up to St Omer to sort out a faulty Spitfire. Pat Patterson flew me up there in an Auster, and I think Doug Clark came for the ride.

We had soon settled in to the 'Hilton' tented accommodation at Carpiquet and got down to the serious business of squadron life. Things were pretty uneventful until one lunchtime when Hank, the sergeant cook for the groundcrew and sergeants' messes, served up a concoction that resulted in everyone who had lunch that day having a bad attack of the 'screamers' – as we referred to diarrhoea.

We were all queuing up at the toilets for the next few days. The toilets consisted of four large buckets, strategically placed, one in each corner of a hessian-surrounded shelter of about six by six-foot square. Very communal and neighbourly under normal conditions, but on this particular occasion things got very fraught. Some chaps made it to the buckets and some didn't. If you got four hefty characters in at the same time who'd taken more than their fair share of Hank's bully beef and beans, it resembled a night at the proms.

Conversation was nigh on impossible and a quiet five-minute read was definitely out of the question. As I said, some made it, some didn't. Proof of the latter was evident for all to see by the number of RAF issue drawers, cotton, airman for the use of that filled the drying lines between the tents.

Enter the two main characters of this little drama, Vic Endacott and Les Synton, both very good radio mechanics on the squadron – but there the similarity ended. They were best friends and shared a tent with four other radio-wallahs. Les was married; Vic wasn't. They were of a similar age, middle 30s, and came from middle-class backgrounds.

Vic was a very clever chap and before the war, due to his multilingual skills, was head buyer at London's Covent Garden fruit market. He was tall, thin and rather lugubrious, until you really got to know him. To go with the heavy horn-rimmed specs, he sported a Groucho Marx moustache. He was well liked and respected by everyone for his intelligence, and he would offer help with any job required.

Les, on the other hand, was totally different. He received the same liking and respect as Vic, but on occasions people's eyebrows were raised. He was a very dapper small man, always the picture of sartorial elegance, even when working. He wore gold-rimmed specs, always had a clean white handkerchief just visible up his left-hand battledress sleeve, and his sparse blond hair was brushed straight back, no doubt with a liberal application of Brylcreem. I never did know what his pre-war occupation had been, but I assumed that because of his uncanny resemblance to Captain Mainwaring of *Dad's Army* fame that he had been a bank manager in some small town where his word would be law.

When, after a hard day's work, we flopped into our 'pits' clad in vest and pants, Les would don his Harrods pyjamas and dressing gown and take half-an-hour on his ablutions before retiring to read for a while. His most treasured possession was his gleaming engine-tuned, chromium-plated and monogrammed Ronson cigarette lighter. Probably a present from a doting maiden aunt! When Les took out a cigarette everyone stopped to watch and witness his precise, fastidious action of lighting it. The Ronson would be plucked daintily from its genuine calf skin pouch, ignited with a reverent gesture and very carefully applied to the selected cork tipped 'Players' in his mouth.

Despite all his breeding, it didn't render Les immune from the now epidemic dose of the 'screamers' that the squadron was enduring and he stood in line as we did to pour out all of his emotions. During the day it was a 'bind' having the urge to visit the latrines so many times, but at night it was literally dicing with death.

Your one aim was to reach the place via the shortest possible route. This, though, was far from easy when the area was a web of guy ropes and concealed tent pegs. There were howls from the occupants when tent pegs were ripped out during the 'fast dash', and then more howls on your return trip if you inadvertently blundered in to the wrong tent and trod on someone's face.

The inevitable then happened. Les had a night attack of the 'screamers'. He set off, picking his way carefully through the tent lines aided by his special miniature torchlight, to arrive safely at the canvas square where he joined the queue already there. His turn came to sit down, but even this was a ritual with Les.

First the bottoms of his Harrods pyjamas had to be carefully rolled up to clear the mud. His dressing gown was then gathered up around his waist, followed by the surreptitious lowering of the pyjamas after careful scrutiny of the wooden inquisition-style contraption they called a seat.

All went well until the final act. Using three carefully folded sheets of regulation form 000 toilet paper, toilet, airman for the use of, he eased himself forward to perform. Suddenly something slipped from the dressing gown pocket, to be followed by a very nasty squelching sound. His gleaming chromium-plated, engine-turned, monogrammed Ronson lighter slowly disappeared beneath the 'you know what'.

He squealed and swore – not profanely, Les would not do that. He gathered up his night attire and hurried carefully back to his tent to seek Vic's advice and assistance on how best to retrieve his most prized possession.

They both emerged some minutes later carrying an assortment of objects deemed necessary to go prospecting for his lighter. A magnet would be useless, even if they had one. Instead they came armed with an assortment of spoons, sticks and even a mess tin. These lads were resourceful and determined.

Without going in to further detail – that's best left to the imagination – the no longer gleaming smoker's requisite was eventually resting in the bottom of the mess tin. During the next few hours it was subjected to much scrubbing, rinsing, wiping and sniffing, until eventually it resembled the item he had unwittingly dropped in to the 'brown stuff'.

Over the forthcoming days this event was the topic of much conversation, though poor old Les took it all in good faith – but it hurt. He never got rid of the smell. Despite drenching it in aftershave and Eau de Cologne, the little genuine calf-skin pouch grimly hung on to its newly-acquired pong and caused passers-by to stare rather strangely at Les whenever he went to light his Players cork-tipped.

To give an insight into life on the squadron during its time in Normandy, here are a few of my diary entries in the days after we got established in France:

27 August 1944
Went into Bayeux – place very badly damaged by RAF and filthy. Once was enough! Caen even worse than Bayeux. Hundreds of dead French and Hun still lying about and under bombed buildings. Town practically a write off. Stench terrible from dead and refuse.

Heard lots of tales of Hun brutality from locals. SS and Gestapo. Snipers still in wood around the airfield. Saw over 4000 dead Huns stacked in a quarry on Falaise road, bulldozers used to compress same then crocodile tank flame throwers used. Unsafe for health reasons to leave bodies lying about and too many to bury. A very grisly sight but none of us felt sorry.

28 August 1944

I and two pals went exploring German shelters. Found grenades, tank mines, ammo and one dead body in khaki. Buried same out of respect. Don't know whether Hun or ours.

Weather very good up till now, but the place has been overrun with insects and flies, practically half the airfield with dysentery and similar complaints from flies and dead bodies. I was one of the lucky ones.

Rumours of a move further up and everybody glad, all getting a bit fed up here. Not enough excitement.

9 September 1944

Move definitely on. 'A' party left, 'B' party follow on when the kites leave. Myself in 'B' party, driving CO's Ford V8. Weather clamped in and we had to stay behind for 2 days. Rained very hard, everybody fed up; moved off 2 days after 'A' party on our first convoy in France!

People cheered and waved everywhere, and we felt pretty good after the hostile reception we first got. Locals were pretty sore about the RAF and the way we had bombed them at Caen and Bayeux. After seeing the same, I don't wonder at it. Uneventful journey, held up 3 hours in R and then carried on to Le Tréport.

10 September 1944

First RAF Wing ever there and entire community turned out first Sunday to see us. Place was like on Ascot day, but the SS were in the district so we had to keep the people away.

Did a roaring trade with locals, 6 eggs for 1 bar of soap, 1 egg for 2 cigs. Local men rationed by Hun to 7 per week. Soap issue even worse, black and heavy as rock.

Got out one night from 6.30 pm and visited town. Place in quite good condition and much cleaner than previous places. Seaside town, people very friendly, asked into tea. Had tea, bread, stewed apples.

More stories of SS cruelty. French buried everything of any value when Hun came in. First taste of French beer. 5F per glass. Quite refreshing but about as strong as Lemonade. Tasted Calvados too! Never again. Bottled TNT!!! Cognac not too bad, but didn't like it. Best drink Liquea Triple Sec. 15F. Very Good.

12 September 1944

Still very busy, drome in a terrible state. Mud everywhere and tents are full of it. Didn't stay long here, about 3 days, and then left in V8 with 2 other squadron trucks for 'L'.

Most interesting journey done by road. Hun trucks, planes and cars everywhere shot up by rocket firing Typhoons. Went through very well-known places of 1914–1918 fame, Arras – Somme – Vimy – Béthune – Abbeville – Pas-de-Calais.

Saw some Buzz bomb sites, also a V2. Also saw a number of last war cemeteries and memorials. Had photo taken by a wrecked engine near Arras. Arrived at the new field [Merville] at 8pm. Place knocked about a little and Hun-damaged main runway.

Joe poses near the wreckage of a train destroyed in an Allied air strike, Arras 1944. The photograph was taken by Flying Officer Hotton, 485 (NZ) Squadron's adjutant. (*Mark Hillier Collection*)

Personnel from 485 Squadron examine a bomb-damaged V1 flying bomb site during the advance across France in the summer of 1944. (*Air Force Museum of New Zealand/Public Domain*)

Chapter 8

Booby Trapped Runway

Life No.3

As the First Canadian Army and other British units were now through Caen and striking north, we were able to follow. Our convoy weaved its way through what was left of Caen over a river bridge hastily constructed by the engineers. The river was full of floating bodies, humans and horses, and as it was August you could imagine the smell.

Eventually we stopped and made camp at what can only be described as a ploughed field. This was Le Tréport. The only memory I have of this place is of all the aircraft tipped on their noses as they tried to taxi over the rough uneven earth. Some Typhoons came off worse and they lost a few pilots this way. The Typhoon would go straight over on to their backs and crush the pilot.

No.485 (NZ) Squadron's armourers' tent, which also doubled as a workshop and office, at Merville in September 1944. Left to right are 'Scotty' (wireless), Joe (fitter), Ricky 'Monty' Norman, who was an armourer, and Frankie Adams, another wireless specialist. (*Mark Hillier Collection*)

This photograph of some of 485's Spitfires in line astern was taken by Max Collett while looking through the gun sight of his Spitfire. Note that they are carrying 50-gallon overload tanks during a sortie that had taken-off from Merville. (*Max Collett*)

Spitfire ML 407, coded 'OU-V', at Merville in September 1944. The aircraft remained with the squadron until just before Operation *Bodenplatte*, at which point she was on loan to 341 (Free French) Squadron having been handed over on 28 December. (*Max Collett, via Peter R. Arnold*)

Joe sat on the wing of the presentation Spitfire *Rangi II*, which was often flown by Warrant Officer Mick Edaile. The original *Rangi* was ML346, coded 'OU-G', which was damaged during operations on 17 July 1944, and duly sent to a repair unit. Note the centre line fuel tank. (*Mark Hillier Collection*)

Flying Officer Terry Kearins, on the left, with Joe on the wing of *Rangi II* at Airfield B35. (*Mark Hillier Collection*)

The aftermath of a force-landing at Merville on 12 October 1944. Joe recalled that he was working on another Spitfire's radiator when Terry Kearins flew right over the top of him and carried out a wheels-up landing. He had been flying Spitfire PT532, 'OU-Q', at the time when it suffered a propeller problem. Yet another close shave for Joe. (*Mark Hillier Collection*)

Another view of Spitfire PT532 on 12 October 1944. (*Mark Hillier Collection*)

The journey up to our next airfield was pretty hectic and made through crowds of French civilians, some waving, and some spitting at us, but they appeared to have not had much suffering at the hands of the occupiers.

We reached our next airfield around 12 September 1944. It was at Merville in France, not too far from Lille. It was a permanent airfield with runways and was supposed to be one of the places the invading German army had chased the RAF expeditionary force from in 1940.

It was getting dark when I arrived, and to crown a long, tiring drive the Fordson finally gave up the ghost. The gearbox and back axle were finished, and after a few grinding yards we got out to find ourselves in the gloom halfway down the main runway.

When daylight came and we returned to retrieve the vehicle, we discovered that both sides of the runway we were stranded on had 500lb bombs equally spaced for the whole length, wired up to be exploded and render the runway unusable. The Jerries' must have left in a hurry before they had chance to detonate them.

Merville was one long unending saga of rain and mud! The tents appeared to be floating and no one had any dry gear the whole time we were there. Rations were good, all supplied by the Army Catering Corps and prepared outside the mess tents over oil and water trap fires.

Occasionally when some intrepid air or ground crew sallied forth armed with .303 rifles we had venison for dinner. I do remember old Hank, the Sergeants' Mess cook, was forever frying eggs by the hundreds. On the odd occasion the sun did come out and a few square yards of the higher ground would dry out, out would come the clothes lines and wet clothing.

Sometimes we visited Lille, about fourteen miles away. It was good to pass through places my father had been in during WW1 – Béthune, Vimy Ridge and the Somme.

On one occasion during our stay at Merville I was working on a Spitfire, on the radiator under the starboard mainplane, when Terry Kearins did a wheels-up landing in 'OU-Q'. He just skimmed over the top of me; I could have poked him with a long stick! He stuck it down on its belly on the grass beside the runway. This I had noted in my diary entry of 12 October. Others around this period illustrate just how difficult and testing the conditions were for us groundcrew trying to service and maintain the squadron's Spitfires in very cold and wet conditions. These are some of them:

September 1944
Used Hun officers' mess as a sergeants' mess. Cigarettes 30 for 10 Francs, beer is 4 Francs a Quart. Lost 1000F at poker so raffled my whiskey. Made 950F on it.

Huns reported all around here. 5 a.m. bombing of Calais, Dunkirk. Ju88 over here two nights running. 5 Canuks knifed in their sleep by SS in civvies. Put a guard round our tents, voluntary.

Went into Lille town on a half day and had my first regular bath over here. Very big city, untouched, went into cathedral. Went to the cinema and watched *In Which We Serve*. Not a bad place, very high priced and practically impossible to buy food.

4 October 1944

Rained very hard, place a sea of mud, tents are flooded, kit soaked. Spent all day digging ditches and trying to drain water away, impossible. Built a bed on 6 petrol tins out of the mud. Feet are soaking, socks wet and no means of drying them out. I have a very bad cold. Managed to wash all my dirty laundry but rained all day so didn't dry.

Went to pictures at night and came back and went to bed with everything wet through. Got fully dressed, greatcoat as well and tried to get warm that way.

5 October 1944

Rain stopped but airfield is 6 inches deep in mud. Still very busy. Hung all laundry out, went to dinner and found same all in the mud.

When I got back, rinsed it all and tried again. Eventually got it dry, sent parcel to England. Lost 500 F at Poker! Went to Armentiers [*sic* – Armentières] with pilots on the beer.

6 October 1944

Best morning for days, sunny, nippy, tons of work. Cold not much better and throat sore. Uneventful day on the whole. Nights getting unbearable under canvas. Just read in paper according to Geneva convention that Italian PoWs moved out of tents into requisitioned houses! Typical!

Saw a wizard Canadian concert party, best so far. 4 WAACs too, first British girls since leaving blighty! Gale!

7 October 1944

Routine! Saw film at night. Saw my first German 'Beetle' robot tank. Cold ok now, fine day and place is drying up.

8 October 1944

Routine, still banging away at Dunkirk!

9 October 1944

Fitted small electric light in my tent.

10 October 1944

More rain and mud, still busy. Dunkirk is taking a great load of bombs, still holding out.

10 October 1944

Went to St Omer to start a kite. Used a car battery and got her going ok. Long run but uneventful. [One of the pilots took Joe in the back of an Auster.]

Rained heavily at 7 p.m. and got soaked again. Finished work at 9.30 p.m. went to mess and drank half a bottle of whiskey. Didn't get drunk, but it prevented me from getting one hell of a cold! Mud everywhere again. Very Busy!

12 October 1944

Nearly bought it about noon as Terry pranged his Kite [Joe was on the airfield close to where the Spitfire arrived in a heap]. Very busy cross wind!!!!!! Dunkirk is in flames.

13 October 1944

Fine cold, very busy. Managed to get a real spring single bed from a Hun store. Gale again and more rain. Tent about to take off any minute.

14 October 1944

Routine. Weather not bad.

15 October 1944

Weather rough, rained hard from 4 p.m. onwards, place deep in mud and water.

16 October 1944

Typhoon lobbed a rocket into our tents. Nobody hurt luckily. Had photo taken in Merville.

17 October 1944

Congratulated for securing German fighter and bomber attack intelligence documents. Same sent to GHQ. Washed all laundry again, just got it hung out and rain came down in sheets. Left it out!!!

18 October 1944

Freak storm at 12 p.m. Tents took off and kites had to be held down. Rain came in sheets and very cold. Gale of 90 MPH and impossible to describe the scene in tent. Just one sheet of water and 5–6″ of soft clay. Had to get up at 10 p.m. to peg the tent down and bale water out. Shoes and kit all floating about.

19 October 1944

Spent most of the day drying kit and tent floor. Dug canals to drain water away. No more rain yet. Very cold wind. Very busy day – Chalky White knocked off a barge! Given up hope of wearing dry socks over here.

24 October 1944

8 p.m. just got back from an 11 hr run with a 3 tonner up into Belgium. We were two mile from the front line. We saw the Commandos mopping up, plenty of fun!

25 October 1944

Max Collet's 21st birthday; 8 bottles of whiskey and 6 gin. Blotto!

26 October 1944

2 months today since we got here. Still busy, weather not bad now. Done the laundry.

2 November 1944

On the move again! Belgium here we come! Crossed into Belgium at 4 p.m.. Arrived at new field at 7 p.m. – about nearest unit to the front line now. Bags of shelling, theirs and ours. Huns everywhere, people very hostile, all pro Nazi. Goodbye to tents at last as we are billeted in a house.

November 1944

Heading north again, this time I was driving the CO's Jeep. We reached our next airfield, Maldegem, in November 1944, situated in Belgium between Bruges and Ghent. It had been a Luftwaffe permanent base.

Our billet though was a large barn-like structure near the small hangar that we had at our dispersal. This hangar was just large enough to house three Spitfires and was used when any big jobs needed doing. There was a fair-sized area of concrete in front of the hangar and perimeter tracks to the aircraft which were parked in rows on the hard earth.

The air crew were billeted in the village of Maldegem, a couple of miles away, and it was all very acceptable.

During its advance eastwards from Normandy 485 (NZ) Squadron had predominantly been deployed in the ground-attack role, hitting anything and everything that moved – trains and motor transport – and gun positions. Joe noted that the squadron was 'happy' carrying out operations from Maldegem – that was until New Year's Day, the last of the Second World War.

Max Collett with his Spitfire Mk.IX at Maldegem – Airfield B65 – in November 1944. (*Max Collett*)

A rare photograph of Joe taken with another member of 485 (NZ) Squadron's groundcrew, Dave Musgrave, at Airfield B65 in November 1944.

Joe with other 485 Squadron groundcrew at Maldeghem in December 1944.

Flight Sergeant Max Collett stands next to his Spitfire Mk.IX NH432, which was coded 'OU-D', at Maldegem. This aircraft was named *Wiapawa Special* after his home town. It was one of the aircraft that were written-off after the Luftwaffe attacks in Operation *Bodenplatte*. (*Max Collett*)

485 NEW ZEALAND SQUADRON

REQUEST THE PLEASURE OF THE COMPANY

OF _____Sgt. Roddis._____

TO

A GRAND BALL

TO BE HELD AT THE

DANCING CERCLE

EEKLOO, BELGIUM.

FRIDAY, DECEMBER 22nd, 1944.

DANCING FROM 18.30 23.00 hrs.

Life on the forward airfields did entail some lighter moments, as this invite to a dance demonstrates. (*Mark Hillier Collection*)

Joe examining the wreckage of a B-17 Flying Fortress, which had been shot over Belgium in 1944, while at Maldegem. (*Mark Hillier Collection*)

As 485 (NZ) Squadron advanced into Belgium they encountered an assortment of abandoned German equipment, such as this Volkswagen Type 166 Schwimmwagen, which gave Joe and the other members of groundcrew something unusual to play with. (*Mark Hillier Collection*)

Another of 485's groundcrew tries out a Luftwaffe inflatable dinghy at Maldegem. (*Mark Hillier Collection*)

DEUTSCHES REICH

ARBEITSBUCH
FÜR AUSLÄNDER

Joe also picked up a number of souvenirs on the Continent, ranging from occupation money through to this passbook for foreign workers. (*Mark Hillier Collection*)

Canadian tanks are seen rolling through the streets of Maldegem in this photograph taken by Flight Sergeant Max Collett. (*Max Collett*)

A fitter and rigger working on the engine of one of 485 Squadron's Spitfires, a presentation aircraft named *Kainui III*. It is likely that this picture was taken at Maldegem in early 1945. (*Air Force Museum of New Zealand/Public Domain*)

Chapter 9

Operation Bodenplatte

Life No.2

The previous night, being New Year's Eve, and with not much happening with the war in our area, we had a noggin or two and had been told not to be too early the next morning. It was very cold and a thick frost lay everywhere. The Spitfires would require defrosting and de-icing.

At about 8 a.m. the groundcrew started to drift out to their aircraft, having had breakfast, to begin their daily routine at dispersal doing pre-flight inspections on the Spitfires which were parked in two straight lines opposite each other. We had not had a visit from Jerry for a while and we were getting too relaxed.

Bill Parker and I came across from the billet, which was a large detached house about twenty yards from our own small blister hangar at dispersal, and, as we rounded the corner of the hangar, were discussing the day's programme, along with the previous night's binge! Half the squadron groundcrew, the advance party and all our airfield defences had gone up into Holland to Gilze-Rijen airfield to prepare the place for our next move and the arrival of the rear party, or us, in a few days.

Two of our aircraft were in the small blister hangar having minor rectifications, while the rest were out on dispersal, as I say being pre-flighted. Obviously with the night before being New Year's Eve, we had all been out on the razzle with the falling down liquid, and as a result were not fully prepared for what happened next.

The sound of aircraft engines made us look up and towards the control tower across the field, but I didn't immediately attach too much importance to it.

We saw three or four aircraft bank round the tower and head towards us in a good line abreast formation. They were pretty low, two or three hundred feet at the most, and coming at us in a shallow dive.

I said to Bill casually, 'The Yanks are out early', thinking they were Mustangs. Then, before he could reply, the front of their wings started to sparkle and flash – and all Hell broke loose as they opened up on our dispersal. The Mustangs had suddenly become Me 109s, and as Bill legged it for the hangar I dived down the side of it, where I knew there was an old air raid shelter. There were already four chaps in there.

Bullets and cannon shells were screaming off the hangar sides and rustling through the camouflage netting. Groundcrew were legging it in all directions; I didn't see Bill again until it was all over thirty minutes later. Some of the groundcrew had been running their

Spitfires, doing magneto and plug checks. They just leapt out leaving the engine running and followed the others to get away from the obvious targets – the Spitfires.

Not being given to emulate an ostrich, after my initial instinctive dash for the shelter I came up for a look see. I was presented with a grandstand view of the shoot-up. Occasionally there would be a clattering and thumping of ammo thrashing along the hangar and camo netting, and I would duck down again, but I had to see this.

The four 109s took turns at coming in, one after the other from different angles, picking a Spitfire and smacking it straight in the cockpit. Most of the Spitfires had full drop tanks on and when hit just exploded in a ball of flame, then sagged in the middle. They all carried one 250lb bomb which they dropped on our dispersal area. One dropped just outside the hangar and the two Spitfires inside were left 'Kaput'. The bombs left a few craters in the earth around the place. They had really caught us with our pants down!

One poor chap was trapped in the toilet which was an open square breeze block type of affair with bricks and a bucket in each corner. He was darting from corner to corner as each 109 came in spraying shells everywhere, but he got out safely.

I watched one of them come down in a shallow dive towards the hangar, pick his Spitfire and destroy it, then bank left over the top of the shelter I was in. As I looked up and to my right, I was presented with a perfect plan view of the banking Me 109. I could clearly see every marking on it, as well as the pilot through the canopy looking back at what he had just done, or maybe looking for another target. We really were sitting ducks as we had no airfield defence.

The pilots by now hearing all the carry on were out in force down in the village. Some still in their pyjamas, all firing whatever they could lay their hands on. Sten guns, Lugers, revolvers – anything that would shoot was used that morning to try and put up some feeble opposition. They could see the airfield was under attack, but they could not see the actual field.

As the 109s turned over the village for another run, the locals were waving and cheering the Luftwaffe – and getting waved back at by the pilots who had obviously been there before.

Eventually, when they had either run out of ammo or fuel was getting low, they disappeared as quickly as they had come. The whole thing was over in about thirty minutes.

The whole wing had suffered from the attack and thirteen of our squadron's Spitfires were write-offs. The pilots arrived and found us doing a salvage job on the un-damaged or slightly damaged aircraft. We had pushed the ones that could be moved away from the burning wrecks. Any aircraft that flew in that day, either to re-fuel or re-arm, were confiscated and by the end of the day we were beginning to get some resemblance of order back.

It was all tied in with von Rundstedt's big push in the Ardennes, but the Luftwaffe suffered more than we did for that last mad fling. It wasn't long before squadrons of Spitfires, Tempests and Mustangs were hot in pursuit to intercept the raiders, now short of fuel and probably out of ammo. According to reports from pilots we chatted to, it was like shooting rats in a barrel. They caught them heading for home with no way of defending themselves. Some of them were very young, inexperienced pilots.

We only lost planes; they lost hundreds of pilots. Squadrons that had not been hit and were actually airborne in the sector at the time of the raids had a field-day. Within days we were back to full strength with Spitfire Mk.IXs and on our way to Gilze-Rijen.

Luckily a few days before the New Year's Day visit from the Luftwaffe, one of our aircraft, ML407, which was coded 'OU-V' and had been with us since Selsey, had been loaned to another squadron which did not suffer an attack and was saved. She later returned to us undamaged.

Hitler's attempt to change the course of the fighting in the West by breaking through the Ardennes to re-capture the port of Antwerp was launched on 16 December 1944. At first the Allies were driven back. Eventually, though, the German advance was halted and it appeared that Hitler's final attempt to break the Allied armies was going to fail. It was thought by the German commanders that the only way the offensive could be resumed was if the Luftwaffe gained superiority of the skies above the battleground. This could only be accomplished if the Luftwaffe threw every available aircraft into the fight. Given the codename Operation Bodenplatte *(or Baseplate) it was Hitler's final chance of achieving some form of victory in the West. As many have described it, it was his, and the Luftwaffe's, last roll of the dice.*

Over 800 fighters and fighter-bombers, predominantly Focke-Wulf Fw 190s and Messerschmitt Bf 109s, were despatched in this low-level attack on Allied airfields in Belgium and the Netherlands. Surprise was complete, as Wing Commander 'Johnnie' Johnson of 144 Wing, at airfield B-56 at Evere, noted in his memoirs, Wing Leader *(Chatto and Windus, London, 1956):*

'I heard the noise of a large number of aeroplanes, but paid little attention, since large formations of American fighters often flew over Evere. Flying along the western boundary of the airfield, the leading elements turned left and the first four Messerschmitts came low over the boundary in loose formation. The cannons belched; the three aircraft behind [Squadron Leader Dave] Harling's Spitfire were badly hit. The pilots jumped from their cockpits and scrambled for shelter. Dave roared down the runway with wide-open throttle. Alone he turned into the enemy fighters and shot one down. But the odds were far too great; our brave pilot was killed before his Spitfire had gathered combat speed ...

'The enemy fighters strafed singly and in pairs. Our few light ack-ack guns had already ceased firing; later we found that the gunners had run out of ammunition. The enemy completely dominated the scene, and there was little we could do except shout with rage as our Spitfires burst into flames before our eyes.'

No.485 (NZ) Squadron was far from alone in being surprised by the Luftwaffe's attacks. At Deurne in Belgium, 193 Squadron was also caught unawares, its Typhoon Mk.Ibs sat helplessly on the ground as the German raiders pounced. One of the squadron's pilots, David Ince, would recall what happened in his book Brotherhood of the Skies *(Grub Street, London, 2010):*

'The sound of diving aircraft came almost as we saw them, a loose gaggle of Me 109s, swarming towards us above the rooftops of Antwerp. Bofors thumped, cannon and machine-guns responded abruptly, and the snarl of engines rose to crescendo as they flashed across the airfield, all mottled camouflage and splashes of yellow.

'In their gunsights were eighty plus Typhoons. Out in the open, most of them fully armed and fuelled. The target of a lifetime. Yet only the first eight carried out any sort of attack. In a single pass they destroyed just one aircraft and caused minor damage to eight others. Two further enemy formations appeared in the circuit. Flying aimlessly around at low level, they made no attempt to avoid the defensive fire, and departed to a cynical chorus of "Weave, you bugger, weave!".'

In the midst of this desperate battle in the Ardennes, a good sense of humour and the ability to make light of any situation would have been a refreshing welcome in that bitter and deadly winter. No.485 (NZ) Squadron's resident cartoonist, 'Ticker' Booth, often recorded events in his drawings, as Joe recalled:

We had a chap with us who I think came to us as a general duties groundcrew chap. We knew him as 'Ticker' Booth. I never knew his first name; he was a quiet chap with a very dry sense of humour.

I knew that he had worked as a cartoonist for a North Yorkshire newspaper – I think it was in Bradford – before the war. Although he was quiet, when he did make light of a situation through his cartoons, they certainly cheered us all up. Normally within hours of a noteworthy squadron event, a cartoon depicting it would appear on the crew room notice board!

Of the events on 1 January 1945, Maldegem had been attacked by Jagdgeschwader 1, its pilots flying a mixture of Bf 109s and Fw 190s. That day, Jagdgeschwader 1 alone lost twenty-five pilots killed or captured. In total, the Luftwaffe lost 143 pilots killed and missing, while seventy were captured and twenty-one wounded. The losses to the Allies were significant, with approximately 232 aircraft destroyed and 156 damaged.

I was feeling quite chipper about the war at that point, it all seemed to be going the right way, although we were still busy. I think we got lazy and our aircraft were not well dispersed as they should have been. The last thing I expected to see was a Jerry aircraft that morning and I certainly was not prepared for what happened.

In retrospect, although as I have said many times before I found the war an adventure and I thought I was very lucky, this was the time that my heart really was in my mouth, what with all that ammo crashing around the place and aircraft going up in smoke around you.

You didn't have time to think then. But I look back and think 'bloody Hell', maybe it was a bit exciting! It certainly focused my thoughts.

I summed things up that day by writing the following in my diary: 'New Years day. Worst day yet. "Strafy New Year".'

The series of cartoons drawn by one of 485 (NZ) Squadron's groundcrew, 'Ticker' Booth, following the events of New Year's Day 1945. Joe recalls that 'Ticker' produced the cartoons soon after the event.

As can be seen, the series, which really needs little description, begins by depicting the planning of Operation *Bodenplatte* by Hitler, Goering, Himmler and Ribbentrop at Berchtesgaden. The next scene depicts Hitler, sitting on an ersatz soap box, briefing his flyers and telling them, 'I don't want any binding about it either', with his subject replying 'Ok my Furore'.

The pilots are then shown getting airborne. One cartoon shows a pilot in his Messerschmitt Me 109 claiming he was happy to be back in the air again after three years, a snipe about the Luftwaffe not having air superiority for so long. The series runs through a typical morning at an Allied base followed by the panic and reactions by the pilots and groundcrew. The last cartoon in the set shows the German pilots as winged avengers and then as angels with harps as they were unfortunate enough to meet a number of Typhoons on the return trip, many being shot down having run out of ammunition.

The series of cartoons was produced for all of the squadron personnel on air ministry paper. 'Ticker' Booth stayed with the squadron until its disbandment, though not much is known about what happened to him after the war. But, as Joe once declared, he was certainly one of 485 Squadron's big characters. (*All Mark Hillier Collection*)

Max Collet standing next to the smoking remains of his Spitfire Mk.IX NH432, *Wiapawa Special*, at Maldegem during Operation *Bodenplatte*. Destruction and smoking wrecks lie all around him. (*Max Collett*)

A general view of the carnage at 485 (NZ) Squadron's dispersal on New Year's Day, 1945. (*Max Collett*)

One of 485's pilots looks on at the devastation at Maldegem during Operation *Bodenplatte*. (*Max Collett*)

One of Joe's snapshots of a 485 Squadron Mk.IX the day after the raid. (*Mark Hillier Collection*)

A Focke-Wulf Fw 190A-8 (*werke nummer* 681497, 'White 11') of 5./JG 4 pictured at St. Trond airfield in Belgium, circa 2 January 1945. This aircraft was flown by Unteroffizier Walter Wagner during *Bodenplatte* on 1 January 1945. Wagner was hit by anti-aircraft fire during the attack over St. Trond airfield. The Fw 190's engine died and he had to make an emergency landing. The picture was taken by a member of the USAAF's 404th Fighter Group which was resident at the airfield at the time. Note how the guns have been removed. (*NARA*)

Members of 485 (NZ) Squadron's groundcrew examining the remains of one of their burned-out Spitfires after Luftwaffe attack on Maldegem, 1 January 1945. (*Air Force Museum of New Zealand/Public Domain*)

Chapter 10

The Advance into Germany

We set off in convoy on an uneventful journey to Gilze-Rijen, which was an airfield between Breda and Tilburg in Holland. I had one minor upset, though, when I nearly overturned the de-icer van I was driving in Antwerp. Trying to take the bend quickly in the centre of town, I skidded and the next minute de-icer tubing and equipment was flying all over the road. But I got away with it, shaken but not stirred.

It was bitterly cold with freezing snow everywhere. V1 buzz bombs were very active and our own artillery was firing over our heads day and night. The Germans were about eight miles away from the airfield and were taking some shifting.

I remember I had a half day off and went to Tilburg with Tom Prickett and saw a film at the ENSA cinema. I also met a friend of mine from my 234 Squadron days, Flight Sergeant Jock Gillespie.

Because it snowed a lot we used to be out at first light clearing the runway. Through February it snowed almost continuously. It was at this time my friend Terry Kearins was posted away from the squadron.

The squadron resumed its normal work which consisted of escorting bombers and also raiding V1 and V2 sites. Our Spitfires could carry a 500lb bombload and our pilots got quite good at attacking these targets.

Once again, my diary entries help reveal what was happening at this point in our war:

8 January 1945
Very cold, all morning packing, crossed the Belgium, Dutch frontier at 15:30 driving a Commer. Had a bad skid and nearly overturned in Antwerp. Hit by a 3-tonner in Breda! New airfield very desolate [Airfield B77]; nearest outfit to front line again, Huns 8 miles away. Bags of action.

9 January 1945
Buzz bombs every half an hour, regular as clockwork. Bags of snow. Artillery quieter tonight and we got a stove fixed up.

10 January 1945
Still banging away. Canadians across the [River] Maas now.

11 January 1945
Not a bad place this. Beautiful scenery; fir trees, snow, people skating. Long walks to meals through the firs. Roll on the day we can go to meals without strapping on the old gun belt.

14 January 1945
Cleared up and very busy. Bags of V1s.

15 January 1945
Artillery at it for 3 hours at 2 am and loads of V1s.

16 January 1945
Very busy and V1s by the dozens, dead overhead.

17 January 1945
Same old thing, more buzz bombs and lots of shelling.

26 January 1945
Misty, more snow. Huns nine miles away now and artillery barrage terrific. Twenty-nine Buzz bombs in just 30 minutes.

During February news of another move turned out to be correct, and on the 25th the squadron headed back to the UK, and, more specifically, Predannack in Cornwall. There it was to re-equip with Hawker Tempests.

On its return to the UK, 485 (NZ) Squadron began the process of converting to the Hawker Tempest. (*Mark Hillier Collection*)

At this point, 485 received a new Commanding Officer, with Squadron Leader Pattison being posted out and Flight Lieutenant Keith Macdonald replacing him. The latter, who arrived fresh from 222 Squadron, had been selected due to his experience of flying the Tempest.

Although seven weeks at Predannack, and with little flying completed, 485's pilots had not warmed to the Tempest. In fact, the decision was taken to re-equip again with Spitfires.

We didn't get very far with the re-equipping programme! We had one old Typhoon and a couple of Tempests to play with, and I got the impression that the aircrew didn't like 'em.

After the Spitfire they were big and heavy. The size of the cockpit didn't go down well, and some said they felt like a 'pea in a bowler hat' sitting in there and that it was like driving a 5-ton truck after a sports car! Although they were faster, stronger and had longer range than a Spitfire, I felt they were not really upset when we returned to Holland without them in mid-April 1945.

Joe and one of his colleagues were not adverse to making a bit of extra money on the side. Knowing that bike tyres were in very short supply on the continent, before departing Predannack they scoured the West Country buying up as many as they could lay their hands on, the intention being to resell them when they arrived back on the Continent.

The squadron duly returned to operations at Twente (Airfield B106) in The Netherlands, taking possession of Spitfire Mk.IXBs, initially as part of 132 Wing. Joe and the ground crew had quite a bit of work to do on these to get them up to the required standard and also had to re-spray the squadron codes on the sides of the aircraft.

Spitfire Mk.IX NH519, an ex 74 Squadron machine, was flown by Max Collett and carried the artwork *Waipawa Special III.* Its last operational sortie with the squadron was on 7 May 1945. (*Max Collett*)

On our return we picked up a full complement of Spitfires left behind by a departing unit and soon had them to our liking. We painted the 'OU's on them all and were just relieved that we didn't have Tempests. The idea behind the re-equip, we heard, was to prepare us for the 3rd Tactical Air Force in the Far East, but we never found out why it didn't happen.

Before leaving Holland, I got permission to take a party to Amsterdam for the day for a look around the untouched City. A good time was had by all. Although we stepped out of the transports on arrival dressed in our best RAF blue uniform, lots of the Dutch thought we were returning Luftwaffe and gave us a hard time.

We had taken all our own day's rations with us packed in a couple of tea chests, and we bunged them into the kitchens of the first decent hotel we spotted. They prepared us a wonderful meal from the food we supplied, which included things that they hadn't seen for years. It was hard work swallowing it though, what with all the hungry faces, inside and out, watching us.

After a pleasant day we headed back to base, only to run out of petrol in a place called Apeldoorn. We managed to locate some in a Canadian Army transport unit and they gave us what we asked for.

Before we left, the CO, a Canadian major, showed us through the base. We ended up at a long, unending row of brick ovens with mountains of ash by each one. It turns out that the place had been a concentration camp. That shook us all.

I had previously visited Belsen with some of the pilots on the way up, but that was a different story altogether. By the time we were allowed near it, they had sanitized it and cleaned it all up, but still with evidence pointing to its infamous role.

On 29 April 1945, we moved on to Drope in Germany as part of 145 Wing. The official identity of the airfield was B105. All the Allied airstrips had 'B' identities for security reasons, but we went by the names as they were easier to remember. Being a permanent camp that had been occupied by the Luftwaffe, we had good accommodation, albeit that we still operated from an open dispersal on the airfield.

After only a couple of weeks here, news of the German ceasefire came through on 8 May 1945. It was eleven months after D-Dy and those first landings in Normandy.

To celebrate we had a football match. I ran in to a barbed wire fence during the game, put my arm up to save myself and ended up with it being bandaged!

Max Collet outside his tent at Drope on VE Day 1945. (*Max Collett*)

Joe sporting the bandaged arm after he ran into a barbed wire fence. (*Mark Hillier Collection*)

Pilot Officer Max Collett had recently survived being shot down whilst at Gilze Rijen, only to nearly come a cropper at Drope in a landing accident – the aftermath of which is pictured here. While he was landing, the propeller of another aircraft behind him sliced through his fuselage up to the cockpit. Max luckily escaped with cuts to his head. This aircraft was a Mk.XVIE, that with the serial number TB741, which was subsequently struck off charge as a Category E write-off. (*Max Collett*)

Max Collet and Russ Clark of 485 Squadron heading home aboard *Andes* in October 1945. (*Max Collett*)

Joe and Max Collet reunited in England. Both men proudly wear the 485 Squadron crest on their blazers.

Chapter 11

Victory in Europe

The fact that war in Europe was really over didn't seem to sink in immediately, but by the end of the day, with all work stopped, the celebrations soon began.

All the messes were thrown open, there was free booze and food, and the mood was set. Old Johnny Dallas, a sergeant rigger from Thurso, had been saving a bottle of Benedictine for this very day and he soon polished it off, even though I had never known him to drink before this point.

As the evening wore on things began to get a bit hectic. Bonfires were lit at the dispersal and when somebody discovered a store filled with artillery shell cases and their contents, they threw them on the fires. Things then got really hot!

I remember at one stage a crowd of us stopping some lads from pushing a Spitfire into one of the bonfires and that really closed down the celebrations. After that, it was little groups of men just standing around and drinking quietly, wondering what would happen to us now?

I remember that the next day a pilot from another squadron took off to do some aerobatics over the field and failed to pull out of a low loop. At the bottom of the loop he went straight through the base of an old windmill nearby. When we got to the scene, we discovered that the fuselage, with him still strapped in it, had gone straight on for about fifty yards, leaving the mainplanes and tail section still wrapped around the windmill. The war had been over for a day and his family would be thinking he was safe now.

It was at Drope that 485 (NZ) Squadron was handed Spitfire Mk.XVIs from another squadron that was departing for the UK.

The squadron had flown over 100 sorties in the last two weeks of the war in Europe, mostly carrying out armed reconnaissance duties. It was from Drope that it undertook its last operational sortie of the war.

Although the fighting in Europe was over, Joe and his colleagues were soon on the move again, though not home, as many had expected – and hoped. Their destination on this occasion, in July 1945, was Airfield B152, another former Luftwaffe base at Fassberg.

There, the squadron received its last Commanding Officer, Squadron Leader Stan Browne. In time, it would fall to him to oversee the squadron's disbandment.

The most important item at Fassberg for me was going on leave, in July, to get married to the girl I had met at the dance at Emsworth. The custom on the squadron when anyone got married was to make a collection, and for me the chaps threw in so many Marks, Francs and Guilders that I could have brought Westminster Abbey for the wedding. At

Acting Squadron Leader Stan Browne can be seen seated in the centre of the front row below the roundel of Spitfire Mk.XVIE which, coded 'OU-J', he flew. He is surrounded by members of the groundcrew. Stan signed the photograph for Joe with the Maori greeting 'Kia ora'. (*Mark Hillier Collection*)

Joe and his wife Mary on their wedding day in 1945. (*Mark Hillier Collection*)

the time, you were only allowed to exchange so much of the 'funny money' (forces notes) for £1 postal orders, though the CO made an exception and allowed me to change the grand total of £100, which was a fair old sum in those days. There was enough left over for the biggest celebration we had ever had.

When I returned from getting married on 14 July 1945, I climbed back into my bunk and found that 'Ticker' Booth had covered one wall with a life-size chalk drawing in colour depicting the wedding ceremony. It was magnificent and I regret not getting a photo of it.

The squadron's days were numbered now, and air and groundcrew were getting posted away every day. The numbers left on the squadron gradually dwindled until, after four-and-a-half years with this family, my turn came at the end of August 1945.

You might get the impression from reading this that I had a wonderful war after joining 485. I did, and even some of the less happy times are fondly remembered. The worst times were obviously when we lost pilots. It affected everyone, some more than others naturally. The groundcrews were very fortunate in that respect and I don't recall losing one 'erk' as a result of enemy action during the time of the squadron's existence. We were all very proud to say we had served with the New Zealanders.

Along with quite a few others, including one of my best mates, Vic Strange, I was given my posting. We duly left Fassberg for Blankenburg transit camp in Belgium. On arrival we were given documents for travel on to our new units – Vic and I were informed that we had been posted to a Mosquito squadron based at Gatwick.

However, a short time later I heard my name being called to the office on the Tannoy. There I was told that due to an admin error, my destination was not Gatwick, but Gatow in Berlin. After a few choking 'cheerios', I was on my way on, beginning a 24-hour train journey to the German capital.

It turned out to be the worst train journey I ever had. Armed with just a blanket and half-a-day's rations, the train set off for Berlin. It was freezing cold, so much so that ice was floating down the Rhine and threatening to damage the road and rail bridges. As a result the train stopped frequently, and its occupants were so hungry, some of the occupants even went into the adjacent fields to pick turnips to eat! I ended up asking the driver of the train if I could ride in the locomotive as it was much warmer than in the carriages. Not an ideal way to start your next posting.

Things, though, got worse, for upon my arrival I was informed that due to a surplus of aero engine fitters in the RAF, I was to be employed in Gatow's motor transport section! Typical RAF. Here was a chap bursting at the seams with Spitfire experience and I was to be employed changing Ford gearboxes. Ah well, it could have been worse.

In time I decided to follow so many of my colleagues and leave the RAF. This I did on 29 May 1946.

Looking back, I am convinced I had a very easy and good war. I attribute this to two things: 1) I always happened to be in the right place at the right time; and 2) I had the good fortune to spend most of the war on a New Zealand Spitfire squadron with air and ground crew whose friendship, comradeship, sense of loyalty, and the appreciation shown to each and every one, was second to none.

Chapter 12

The Cold War RAF

I served nearly 3 years in the 'G' reserve during which time I did a two-year apprenticeship at Moore & Wrights in Sheffield as a machine-tool maker and setter. At the time, my wife and baby daughter were living with my parents in one room of their house in Sheffield, waiting to get on to the Council housing list. This never seemed to be getting any nearer, and after long discussions with my wife and family I finally convinced them that by going back into the RAF we would quickly get into the married quarters.

So it was that I re-joined the RAF in November 1948, this time as a Leading Aircraftsman Engine Fitter. My sergeant rank at demob, like all other wartime promotions, was only temporary.

Mary and our baby daughter went to live with her sister in Manchester, while I was sent to RAF Abingdon in Oxfordshire. On arrival there my medical exam decided that varicose veins on both my legs needed seeing to and for the first time in my life, I went into hospital and had them sorted. This got me a week's leave over Christmas. Good start!

Having recovered from the operation, Joe was soon back in the thick of it, this time becoming involved in a humanitarian crisis. After the end of the war, Berlin, like the rest of Germany, had been divided into sectors, each controlled by one of the victorious Allies – Britain, the US, France and Soviet Union. In time, the wartime alliance between the Western Allies and the Soviet Union ended and relations turned increasingly hostile.

Stalin's Soviet Union sought to drive the Western democracies from Germany to continue the communist advance across Europe. The first step in Stalin's scheme was to bring Berlin under Soviet control. The Soviet leader decided to make the Allied hold on West Berlin untenable by shutting down all the overland routes used to keep the city supplied – orders for which he gave on 24 June 1948.

The choice faced by the Allies was a stark one – let Berlin fall, or risk war with the Soviets by breaking the Eastern Bloc's stranglehold. In response, in what was a remarkably visionary move, the Allies decided that they could keep Berlin supplied by flying over the Soviet blockade, thus avoiding armed conflict with the USSR.

What has come be to known at the Berlin Airlift began on 26 June 1948. Throughout the following thirteen months, more than 266,600 flights were undertaken by the men and aircraft from the US, France, Britain and across the Commonwealth. These missions between them delivered in excess of 2,223,000 tons of food, fuel and supplies in the greatest airlift in history.

On my return to Abingdon I was put to work on the Avro York. This aircraft was to be used extensively in the Berlin Airlift. I was initially working on the aircraft in the hangar at Abingdon, working on the Rolls-Royce Merlin engines. The RAF code-name was Operation *Knicker*, and it was on 25 June 1948, that the British started ferrying supplies into RAF Gatow from Wunstorf in just six Dakotas from Nos. 38 and 46 Groups, Transport Command. More aircraft were on their way, and the first reinforcements arrived on 25 June.

I was soon despatched to Wunstorf itself to work on the aircraft there. It was hard work and entailed long hours. A three-shift system – 6 a.m. to 2 p.m.; 2 p.m. to 10 p.m.; and 10 p.m. to 6 a.m. – was introduced. I had one or two trips home when Yorks went back to Abingdon for servicing.

So quickly did the RAF's involvement in the Berlin Airlift escalate that Wunstorf soon became so crowded with RAF personnel that even attics in a number of the buildings in the area were converted into huge dormitories.

As the aircrews that had arrived at Wunstorf flew into Gatow to familiarise themselves with the routes into West Berlin, the British Army took over the Control Commission's civilian food team for Lower Saxony and began to assemble the goods required for the first lift, scheduled, as we have seen, for 28 June 1948. On that day, and for the following two days, the Dakotas flew twenty sorties from Wunstorf to Gatow, carrying seventy-five tons, mostly of food, for the British troops.

Initially, based on an estimate of the needs of West Berlin, it was calculated that 4,500 tons of varied goods was the minimum daily requirement. Soon the Dakotas were moved out to make way for the Avro Yorks which could carry more.

This picture, one of a series detailing Joe's service in the Berlin Airlift, shows one of the RAF's Avro Yorks at Wunstorf. Joe can be seen standing beside the port undercarriage. (*Mark Hillier Collection*)

LAC Joe Roddis poses for the camera besides one of the Yorks at Wunstorf. (*Mark Hillier Collection*)

Groundcrew pictured on the engine nacelle of an RAF York at Wunstorf. (*Mark Hillier Collection*)

A crane is manoeuvred alongside a York in one of the hangars at Wunstorf in preparation for an engine change. (*Mark Hillier Collection*)

The replacement engine sits on the hangar floor prior to being fitted to the York (*Mark Hillier Collection*)

The old engine is lifted off the York as Joe and his colleagues proceed with its replacement. (*Mark Hillier Collection*)

RAF groundcrew snatch a moment's rest during the York's engine replacement at Wunstorf. Joe can be seen in his coveralls on the right. (*Mark Hillier Collection*)

Maintenance personnel photographed by Joe on a David Brown aircraft towing tractor in a hangar at Wunstorf. Weighing nearly four tons and powered by a David Brown four-cylinder, 2,523cc, overhead-valve petrol engine, these tractors were a common sight on RAF airfields throughout the Second World War, and in some instances remained in service until the 1970s. (*Mark Hillier Collection*)

An Avro York landing at RAF Gatow during the Berlin Airlift. (*Historic Military Press*)

To keep a city of more than 2 million people functioning required an enormous variety of goods to be delivered to it on a regular basis. The airlift began as a food supply service, and food remained the most important of the goods transported throughout the months of the Soviet siege.

The official British account of the airlift recorded that when the airlift was operating at its highest level, the RAF delivered the following: a) Food and other supplies for the British garrison at a rate of forty tons per day; b) Food for the civilian population totalling 1,300 tons per day; c) Coal, mostly for essential services such as the maintenance of the public utilities (electricity supply, sewage disposal, hospitals etc.) and for the furnaces of factories. Other than this, there was a small allowance for domestic heating; d) Liquid fuel, mostly petrol for motor transport and diesel oil for heavy transport and power plants; and e) Special freight.

Special freight fell into three categories. The first of these was newsprint. Strange though it may seem, this was a vital commodity. Newspapers were the principle means of communication, and keeping the Berliners informed was essential for their morale. With electricity supplies limited, many evenings had to be spent in the dark, this the Berliners could endure but being kept in the dark regarding what was happening to and across their city would have proved intolerable. It is interesting to note, with regards to paper and newsprint, that more newspapers were sold in Berlin during the Soviet blockade than had been the case for many years.

The next category of special freight was that termed as 'economic freight'. In simple terms, this was the raw materials necessary for industry to function, without which there would be mass unemployment bringing with it even greater hardships than the citizens were already suffering. The third part of the special fright was all the other items which enabled a city to function, such as medical goods and children's shoes.

While targets were set of the required quantities of each category of these goods, there was a degree of flexibility in the numbers to allow for changing circumstances. An example of this was with coal and the weather. Though the aim was to deliver enough of each key commodity to accumulate thirty days' reserve stocks and then maintain them at those amounts, a change in the weather, for example, could seriously affect these levels. So, in particularly harsh weather conditions, the consumption of coal for heating purposes would increase considerably. In such circumstances, more of the available flights would be switched to carrying coal.

By contrast, if those airfields dedicated to the transport of coal were cloaked in fog for extended durations and flights were grounded, every effort would be made to build up supplies of other items from the other airfields. When the better weather returned, the main effort of the aircraft would be concentrated on delivering coal, knowing that the other items could be ignored for the time being because of the large stocks that had been built up of those goods.

The air-bridge eventually became so effective that more supplies were delivered to Berlin during the blockade than had previously been shipped overland. Stalin increasingly saw that his bid to seize control of the German capital would never succeed. Bowing to the inevitable, at one minute after midnight on 12 May 1949, the Soviet blockade was lifted. It was an event that Joe was rightly proud to have been part of.

When the airlift finished, Mary and I still did not have a home of our own, so I made a few enquiries at Wunstorf. I found out that if I stayed on in Germany I would get a

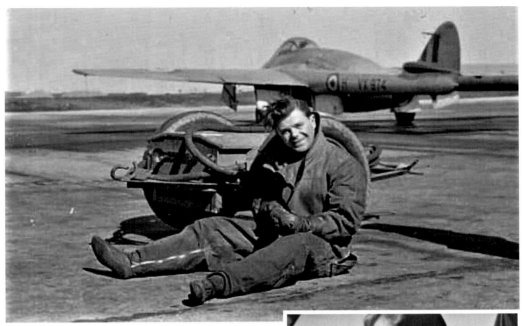

Joe pictured in front of a 2 Squadron
DH Vampire FB5 at RAF Gütersloh
in 1950. (*Mark Hillier Collection*)

Joe carrying out an engine run in the cockpit
of an Avro York at Wunstorf during the
Berlin Airlift. (*Mark Hillier Collection*)

Joe on top of a DH Vampire of 3 Squadron, carrying out maintenance on the Goblin 2 engine in Germany.
(*Mark Hillier Collection*)

This trio is, from left to right, a Corporal Armourer known as 'Jock'. Joe Roddis, then an engine fitter, and Corporal Phillips. The photograph was taken at RAF Sylt whilst 3 Squadron were on camp. On the reverse Joe had written 'For air firing range – we were more interested in the nearby nudist beach. The suit I am wearing was for working inside or outside AVTAG fuel tanks'. (*Mark Hillier Collection*)

A Corporal again, having started back at Leading Aircraftman, Joe is seen here as he fills up a tanker at RAF Gütersloh whilst with 3 Squadron. (*Mark Hillier Collection*)

Second from the right, Joe and other members of groundcrew pose for the camera with one of 3 Squadron's pilots at RAF Sylt, April 1950. (*Mark Hillier Collection*)

married quarter much quicker. This I discussed with Mary, she approved and I volunteered to do a tour in Germany.

I was posted to RAF Gutersloh to 3 (Fighter) Squadron equipped with Vampires, which were powered by the de Havilland Goblin engine. I attended a course on the Goblin at de Havilland at Hatfield, and, on my return, I was informed there was a married quarter available for me. My family moved in just before Christmas 1948; we were very happy to be together in our own place at last.

No.3 Squadron also had a Meteor T7 for aerobatic displays and I had a few rides in that with a pilot who lived quite near me in our married quarter. We had some wonderful family holidays while we were there, visiting places such as Hamburg, Osnabrück and Sylt.

On completion of my tour I returned to the UK with my family in 1951, being posted to RAF Cosford. I was to be an instructor in my trade at the School of Technical Training.

At the end of the posting I was promoted back up to sergeant (substantive). Before leaving Cosford I took advantage of the trade structure and by completing a five-day exam at RAF St Athan I passed out as a senior technician and turned my three stripes upside down and got more pay!

By now it was 1953 and we were on the move again, this time to RAF Marham in Norfolk. There they had Boeing B-29 Washingtons, four squadrons of them – 35, 135,

Joe is seen here seventh from right in the rear row after completing a technical course at RAF Cosford in September 1951. (*Mark Hillier Collection*)

207, and 214 (tankers). I was posted to 207 Squadron. I attended a long course at Marham on every trade and aspect of the B-29 and passed.

I was on the dispersal on the far side of the airfield, sharing the aircraft with another crew chief. Whenever the aircraft left the UK, the crew chief flew with it. This was due to the fact that wherever they landed overseas it was unlikely there would be any tradesman present who knew much about the B-29.

I flew at the Queen's review over RAF Odiham on 15 July 1953. Being the largest aircraft in the flypast, we were the first and slowest past the saluting base.

On one occasion we went on detachment to Saibah, near Basra in Iraq, on standby as a backup with spares for two RAF Canberras involved in a London to New Zealand air race. On our return to the UK we were diverted to Habbaniya to help relieve gridlock at a transit camp there for forces returning home. All the Hastings transport aircraft had been grounded with a technical problem and we took about a dozen soldiers' home.

At this stage we were awaiting re-equipment with the Canberra and all the B-29s had to be flown back to the USA for storage at Tucson in Arizona. We lost one aircraft and all its crew on its flight over to America – it was a 35 Squadron aircraft, I think.

I remember reading the accident report. The aircraft had taken off on Monday, 25 January 1954, with its pilot being one Flight Lieutenant Williams. It took off from Prestwick en-

Pictured inside the American Air Museum at Duxford, Joe is standing beside a Boeing B-29, which in RAF service was the Washington. This was a type that Joe often flew in as a Crew Chief. (*Mark Hillier Collection*)

route to the Azores. Sometime later an R/T message was received which stated that the aircraft was experiencing 'fuselage vibration and severe icing' and that they were turning on to an easterly heading. Not many minutes later a further garbled message was received which sounded like 'baling out'. This was the last message received from WF495. It was initially thought the crew had baled out or ditched in the Morecambe Bay area. Despite an extensive search, nothing was found and the crew were posted as missing.

We gradually received our Canberras and got on with familiarisation. As we had been doubled up as crew chiefs on the B-29, we now had a surplus of senior NCOs and I, along with some of the others, was posted to RAF Binbrook which had four squadrons of Canberras.

There I was put in charge of the engine change and repair section. I had an area at one end of the hangar housing about a dozen new Rolls-Royce Avons, all new and straight from the factory in cradles and crated. It was a sizeable workshop with a dozen or so very good fitters. We did the entire engine, jet pipe and large component changes for all the aircraft at Binbrook.

If a Canberra was forced to land away from base with a technical problem, either home or abroad, I was sent to determine the cause and inform the engineering officer at Binbrook. I would inform him what I required, from a replacement engine through to any other component, even if it was from a different trade, how many men I needed to do the job, and then get the aircraft back to base as soon as possible.

I would then remain there, sort out accommodation and wait for the arrival of the new engine and my team. I'd do as much as I could whilst waiting. This might be getting the unserviceable engine ready for removal by just leaving the main bearer bolts in. Some jobs took a day, a week or even a month, delays often being due to waiting for the replacement parts to arrive. But we always got the aircraft home.

Sometimes I was flown out to the location in a Canberra of the squadron whose aircraft I was going to work on, sometimes it was a civilian flight. It was a peach of a job. In my absence, the sergeant in the section would often go, just to give him a share of the good jobs.

At that time, the Binbrook squadrons came in for their share of doing a stint in the Far East, being stationed at RAF Butterworth, Penang. Their job there was atatcking the Malayan National Liberation Army.

As early as the 1920s, Communist Soviet and then Chinese agents had been infiltrating Malaya. Then in 1929 the Malayan Communist Party, or MCP, was formed with the intention of overthrowing the Malayan Administration and establishing a Communist-controlled democratic republic. After the end of the Second World War, the MCP revived its original aims through peaceful means but found little popular support amongst the Malayans. So the Communists turned to violence.

By the summer of 1948 the scale of insurrection was such that Emergency Powers were invoked by the Federal Government on 16 June, and the military authorities were called in to assist the civil administration in restoring law and order – and this included units from the RAF, RAAF, RNZAF, and the local auxiliary and national air forces. The difficulties of operating in a country the size of England and Wales, of which 80 per cent is dense jungle, against a mobile force of less than 10,000, were immense.

The RAF's involvement operated under the codename Operation Firedog. A number of different RAF squadrons were involved in the Emergency, which lasted until 1960, using types such as the Spitfire, Avro Lincoln, Vampires, Mosquitos, Dakotas and Canberras, amongst others.

Of the four Canberra squadrons at Binbrook, 9 and 12 had done their tour in the Far East, so soon it came to be 617 Squadron's turn to go. I was chosen to go with them [in July 1955]. We had a gruelling flight out to Butterworth in a Hastings that travelled via Habbaniyah, Karachi, Negombo, and Singapore to reach Penang.

We loved it. It was hard, hot work and too hot to do anything by noon, so we were free to do our own thing in the afternoon. Nearing the end of our stint there we got the dreaded fuel bug.

Within a week of relieving 12 Squadron at RAF Butterworth our Canberra aircraft were doing what they had been designed for – dropping 500lb bombs. Serviceability of the aircraft was good, and the flying hours were building up at a steady rate for the first couple of months. Then things stated happening; little niggling things to start with, but then it got considerably worse!

It started with the throttles which wouldn't synchronise. The CO returned from a sortie one day with an unacceptable degree of throttle stagger and no amount of normal rectification seemed to work. He would take-off with a slight difference in the throttles

In this photo of 617 Squadron groundcrew at RAF Butterworth Joe can be seen second from the right. Note the canopy shades to keep the cockpit cool. (*Mark Hillier Collection*)

for a synchronised [one throttle lever for each engine] RPM and then return with the throttles set up to three inches apart, and nothing we did seemed to cure it.

We changed every unit in the fuel system with varying success, but, in the end, had no joy with eliminating the problem. It just got worse.

In a short space of time all of the aircraft were returning with throttle stagger or, worse, they started losing an engine, and even experienced flame-outs at altitude or compressor stall. Things were getting very fraught. The situation was getting dangerous and we couldn't rectify it. I removed a throttle spindle and found it badly scored.

When flight commander Flight Lieutenant John Cochrane – later to become number 2 to Brian Trubshaw on Concorde flight testing – lost both engines, but managed to re-light one of them and return safely, it was time for serious action. We grounded all the aircraft and called for the Binbrook Rolls-Royce representative, Jack Dyke. Jack tried some of his own theories, including checking the high-pressure fuel pump output pressure, but when he removed a throttle spindle and saw the number and depth of the scores along its entire length, he knew what to do. On his authority the famous Dambusters were grounded.

Jack resolved the problem by sending fuel samples to Rolls-Royce in Derby. On receipt of the results we could have all been forgiven for thinking it was 1 April. The cause of all our problems stemmed from the antics of a 'bug' invisible to the naked eye and which was living in the fuel tanks at Butterworth. Every time our aircraft were refuelled, we were just adding to our problems.

According to Jack Dyke, informing us from in his report, this bug took in AVTAG [a type of fuel] at its front end, which then passed through its body to emerge at the other end as near pure sulphur. The sulphur, once in the Avon fuel system, attacked the special metal coating of the high-pressure fuel pump plunger slipper pads. This caused corrosion and pitting which scored the facing of the pump swash plate and particles of the detached metals were held in suspension in the fuel. The amount of fuel reaching the engine was controlled by a fuel servo system. The servo system itself was controlled by the various fuel system components which catered for altitude, forward speed and acceleration (throttle opening).

The progressively variable ram for correctly positioning the inlet guide vanes to the low-pressure compressor had its own fuel pump, but it still fell victim to the dreaded bug. In the individual fuel system components, the build-up, or release of servo pressure was determined by the position of a very positive and precise item referred to as the half ball valve. Particles of metal in suspension became embedded in and under the valve causing an incorrect signal at the fuel pump therefore reducing fuel flow to the burners.

We removed all the Avons completely and drained and flushed the aircraft fuel tanks. We took no more supplies from Butterworth's fuel tanks.

Rectification got underway quickly – we all wanted to be home for Christmas, and time was running out. Each aircraft's fuel system and tanks were thoroughly purged and re-filled with clean fuel.

All fuel was now flown in from Changi, in Singapore, and all fuel system components and some engines were changed. Ground runs followed to make sure everything was working, followed by a satisfactory air test on each airframe.

We were ordered back to Binbrook and the all clear given to go home. I'm not positive just how many aircraft we had in the detachment, probably eight or ten, but they all left for Nogombo, while we, the groundcrew, were to follow in our old friend, the Hastings. I was instructed to stay with the rear party to get them all home. Clean up behind if you like.

On arrival at Nogombo we saw no Canberras on the ground. However, our next stop was Karachi Muripur, where we had one on the apron. The pilot had an ancillary problem which had partly been rectified by the station flight, and the aircraft left the next morning just ahead of us on the leg to Habbanyah.

Half-an-hour into the flight and our Hastings did a 180-degree turn and headed back to where we had just come from – the Canberra was having trouble and was returning. The pilot had experienced acceleration problems and slight oil pressure fluctuations with the port engine. The acceleration control unit was replaced and adjusted and the scavenged oil filter removed, inspected and cleaned before being refitted. The ground test went ok, and off he went to air test it. Just as we boarded the Hastings to take-off, the Canberra appeared back in the circuit making ready to land.

Apparently, he had lost the starboard engine half-an-hour after departure. It seems the engine just wound down and a single engine landing was inevitable. We all stood and watched and waited along with the emergency teams. He was rather high on his final approach and was halfway down the runway when he touched down. He attempted a go around and slammed the throttle on the good port engine forward. We heard it accelerate to maximum RPM, but the port wing lifted and the starboard wing tip overload fuel tank touched the runway. The port engine throttle was closed, and the aircraft slammed back onto the runway causing the landing gear to collapse and he ended up in one piece ahead of a trail of debris. That Canberra was left on the runway and we departed again for Habbaniyah.

As we arrived overhead we observed five Canberras on the apron, line abreast all looking unserviceable. There was no activity at all around them and it looked bad. On landing we were told that the dreaded Butterworth bug had struck again, and that they had all experienced similar engine problems. Home for Christmas was now looking decidedly dodgy.

A signal from Binbrook informed me that replacement engines would be delivered to us as and when air transport become available. We were to change the engines on receipt of same, prepare the lame ducks for return to Binbrook and the aircraft that brought the replacements would carry out full purging of the fuel tanks and cleansing of the aircraft fuel systems.

We moved the five Canberras off of the concrete apron onto the sand to make way for visiting aircraft and set about preparing the engines for removal down to the bare bolts. That done we purged and flushed the aircraft fuel systems and tanks. We then put on all of the appropriate covers and protectors on to sand proof the aircraft, then just waited.

The new Avons came to us in ones and twos aboard Avro Yorks and Handley Page Hastings. Finally, just over a month later the last lame duck was back in the air heading for home.

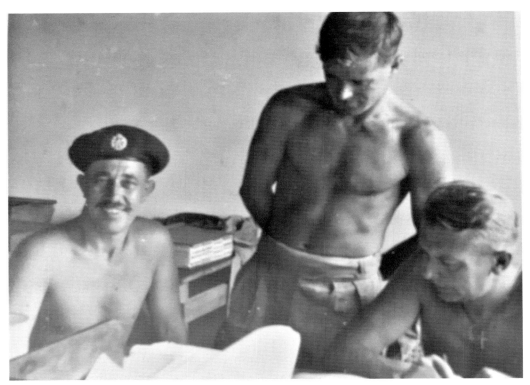

In 617 Squadron's engineering office at RAF Butterworth are, left to right, Sergeant Reynor, Joe, and Warrant Officer Foster. (*Mark Hillier Collection*)

Standing on the right, Joe is seen here with a few of his groundcrew colleagues from 617 Squadron in front of the accommodation at RAF Butterworth. (*Mark Hillier Collection*)

During one of the waiting days at the airfield I was flown to Shaibah to rectify a small engine problem on a 207 Squadron Canberra from Marham. It had diverted there whilst on a routine overseas exercise flight. I got him away ok and later learned he reached Marham safely. We were glad to see the back of these issues and had a trouble-free flight back in the Hastings to RAF Binbrook.

We did eventually get home and were so glad to see our families at Binbrook at last. No.617 Squadron was the last squadron to do the Butterworth detachment as the Royal Australian Air Force took over.

Eventually all good things come to an end and in October 1959 I was selected to go for aircraft servicing chief (crew chief) training on the first of the V-bombers, the Vickers Valiant. It lasted some months, covering again all trades and it was at some horrible camp in Wiltshire. We were back living in Nissen huts with coke burning stoves – terrible in mid-winter.

It was a long slog back home at the weekends, as my family were still at Binbrook. I passed the course with a great bunch of chaps, at which point the time came for posting. Where did I go? Back to 207 Squadron at Marham, at the very same dispersal pan that I had been at with the B-29! I arrived and banged in my request for married quarters and set about putting into practice what I had been taught.

On the far right wearing his flying suit, Joe is seen here while he was Crew Chief on the Valiants of 207 Squadron at RAF Marham, with which he would often fly on detachment. (*Mark Hillier Collection*)

I took over Valiant WZ404 from one of its two crew chiefs and carried out my job with the initial help of the other one. They were big, even bigger than Avro Yorks, but they were beautiful. We had a great aircrew and as soon as I became fully confident with the aircraft, I became eligible to go on Eastern and Western rangers.

Like the B-29, when the aircraft left the UK, or was to attend displays, the crew chief flew with it. The Eastern jobs were all over the place, even as far as Zimbabwe, while the Western ones to the USA. We were now in SACEUR, or Strategic Air Command Europe, carried the nuclear deterrent and visited headquarters of Strategic Air Command at Offut, a base in Omaha, Nebraska.

We also started QRA, or Quick Reaction Alert, for a week at a time living with the aircraft on a spare, secure enclosed base away from the main camp. We were infested with 'ban the bomb' ladies incessantly, and when not on QRA with the aircraft I spent my time helping to pull screaming females off the chain link fencing around the QRA side of the airfield.

There were three Valiant's on QRA (214 Squadron didn't do it they were flying tankers), one from each of the three bomber squadrons. I was in my element there. My family didn't go much on it, except when I arrived home with arms full of cigarettes, bananas and pineapples, but they put up with it, bless them.

Eventually it all ended abruptly. The main spar of the Valiant suffered metal fatigue with the result that all aircraft were scrapped.

I was posted to Gaydon. They had a Vulcan, a Victor and a few other jobs there, but too many redundant crew chiefs wandering about, so I elected to help with the gliding fraternity, maintaining the gliders and flying them on a Wednesday afternoon and weekends. After a while I got fed up with this way of life and volunteered for a Victor PRU (Photographic Reconnaissance Unit) squadron that was being formed, but I didn't get it.

Against this backdrop, in 1965 I took the decision to leave the RAF. Such were my skills that I quickly got a good job at the Rolls-Royce aero engine department in Derby. I had joined the RAF at 17 and left at the age of 44. I loved every minute – nearly!

The family were now living in a house we rented in Kings Lynn, something that we had arranged before we left Binbrook. Whilst I was at Rolls-Royce I spent all my spare time looking for a house to buy for the family to live in. We now had a daughter, who was born in 1947, Kathleen Mary, and a son, Joseph Martin, who was born in Ely's RAF hospital in 1954 while we were at Marham.

I enjoyed my time at Rolls-Royce on engine testing, working with development engines. I did not want to go on the production side of the job. The RB211-06 was in now and I enjoyed the variety of jobs, especially the stripping of components after each test to check for wear.

After a couple of years I got the chance to go on the staff as a specification engineer on the RB211-22. I was eventually promoted to section leader, then senior specification engineer. I was happy again, and worked on the RB211-24 and the Trent Engines at their beginning.

I made some wonderful friends there, but when they introduced computers to take over a lot of my work I didn't approve. I stuck it for a while and did the odd spot of key tapping, but I eventually decided that I'd had enough, took a hand shake and pension, and retired in 1962 at the age of 61.

We had a lovely home in Derby and I had plenty of hobbies. This included a bit of DIY, caravanning, fishing – you name it, I did it and couldn't get enough of it. In time, Kathy left home and married, living in Norfolk. My son eventually followed suit, leaving Mary, I and the dog to rattle about in a three-bed semi in Derby.

In 2000, my wife Mary, who had not been well for a while, was diagnosed with a brain tumour. It was inoperable and she was given five to six months to live. She very seldom complained, but in the later stages she really suffered. She died in her sleep on 22 May 2001.

In 2004, I was asked to appear in a documentary called *Spitfire Ace* involving the ex-485 Squadron Spitfire ML407. Carolyn Grace had been asked if she knew of any groundcrew who were on 485 (NZ) Squadron with her aircraft. For some reason, she gave them my name.

Little did I know that Betty was to see me on the TV. I had last seen at the dance in Worthing in 1944. She was now living in Selsey, West Sussex, in a flat on her own since her husband had died. Her grandson, Lawrence, saw that the programme was on and knew Betty had been involved with Spitfires, phoned her and told her to turn on Channel 4.

Who should she see on the screen at that precise moment? Yours truly! She didn't recognise me, but my name was on the screen and she said, 'I know him'. After some

Pictured at a supporters' event for ML407, Joe is second from the left. On the far left is Battle of Britain veteran Wing Commander Bob Foster DFC AE. Carolyn Grace is on the right. (*Mark Hillier Collection*)

persuasion by her family and a friend, Betty was encouraged to write to Channel 4 and ask for my address. Channel 4 wouldn't divulge this information, but said if she wrote me a letter, they would pass it on.

I duly received her letter, sat on it for about two weeks and then phoned her one evening. We continued phoning regularly and I told her I would like to visit her in Selsey.

I arrived in Chichester one afternoon by rail – and there she was at the platform. For me it was magic. Even though sixty years had passed, she was the same Betty to me, the same Betty that I had last seen on that railway platform at Worthing some six decades earlier.

I stayed with Betty for a couple of weeks and met her family and friends. I was reluctant to return to Derby. Two more visits followed, each longer than the last and then I asked how she would feel about me moving down to live with her. She was all for it. I put my house up for sale, all the contents, down to the last tea spoon, threw my Ford Escort in for good measure and got my asking price!

I moved to Selsey in 2004 at the start of what were to be eight of some of the most wonderful years of my life. We had great holidays in Portugal, on the Isle of Wight, to Devon, Wales and many other places. I was 83, Betty was 84, so we didn't do much dancing, although she could still trip the light fantastic all day if you let her.

After about five years Betty sold the flat and we bought a bungalow in the same road dead opposite. She had always wanted to live in a bungalow and it was perfect. We were both

Joe and Betty at Goodwood having just been flying in the Cap 10 behind with Mark Hillier. Betty also had a flight in a Piper Cub. (*Mark Hillier Collection*)

still very active and lived life to the full. We both appeared in TV documentaries, including one with David Jason about the Battle of Britain, and another with John Sergeant about Spitfires. We were very, very happy. We went everywhere together, she was very special.

One morning in February 2012, she complained of feeling sick and very unwell. This came out of the blue. Her son-in-law, Alan, and daughter, Linda, called an ambulance. They took her in to Chichester hospital and she was diagnosed as having a ruptured ulcer in her stomach. She was given a 50/50 chance of survival. She had an operation at 8 p.m. that night but went on to a life support machine shortly afterwards. With the family's agreement, it was switched off just after midnight on 1 April 2012.

Words can't describe my feelings. I never thought I would lose her by out living her – she was so strong and active. Life can be so cruel.

Epilogue

By Mark Hillier

In the years after Betty's passing, Joe continued to be actively involved with aviation, often being seen at Tangmere Military Aviation Museum, regularly flying at Goodwood or attending reunions at Bentwaters with ML407 at the request of the Grace family. He also attended signings and loved to meet aviation enthusiasts to share his experiences and chat about the war.

Joe even completed a parachute jump for his favourite charity at the age of 90. He was always keen to share his knowledge and experience gained through years of service in the RAF and with Rolls-Royce at Derby. Loved and cherished by many, wherever he went he held court and loved to chat.

At the age of 91, Joe was asked by the Boultbee Flight Academy (now Spitfires.com) if he thought he could start and run up their Mk.IX Spitfire at Goodwood. There was no stopping him, and, with little hesitation, as well as a crowd watching, Joe fired up the Merlin. He ran up G-ILDA, at one of the airfields he had served at with 485 (NZ) Squadron back in 1943. A memorable moment for all.

Sadly at the age of 94 Joe's health began to deteriorate. Nevertheless, he was still determined to get out and about and talk aviation. Even the week before his death, he attended the museum at Tangmere for a wander round with my young son in tow, or maybe it was the other way around?

Joe's funeral was held at Chichester Cemetery. It was a full house, with his son Martin and family, along with many friends and family, including pilots and aviation enthusiasts from all over, present. One airline pilot come all the way from Australia. Among the mourners was his old friend Peter Hale of 41 Squadron, who had flown Mk.XII and Mk.XIV Spitfires; the two of them had formed a special bond and enjoyed mutual respect, although Joe was not one to hold back on giving Peter a hard time with his sharp wit from time to time. Carolyn Grace was also present.

The day passed with a final salute by one of Boultbee Flight Academy's Spitfires, flown for the occasion by Matt Jones, and a Harvard aerobatic display by Goodwood Flying School over the wake. A great tribute to an amazing man. I for one will miss him greatly!

Blue Skies Joe!

Joe and Peter Hale together for one last reunion at Sywell during an ML407 supporters' club gathering. Warrant Officer and Chief Technician, pilot and ground crew, they often bickered, but were firm friends. Between them they had some hair-raising stories and it was always fascinating listening to them. They are standing next to a Hispano Buchon that, used in the filming of *The Battle of Britain*, is being restored to flying condition by Richard Grace. (*Mark Hillier Collection*)

Joe sat on the wing of Spitfire G-ILDA at Goodwood after having just started her up. It was the first time since the Second World War that he had done so on a Spitfire, and he proved that he had not forgotten a thing. (*Mark Hillier Collection*)

Joe holding council with a few of the pilots at Goodwood Aero Club on the occasion of his 94th birthday. (*Mark Hillier Collection*)

Joe sat in the cockpit of Harvard IIB G-AZSC getting ready to go. (*Mark Hillier Collection*)

Joe taking off for what would turn out to be his last ever flight, although at this time he was fairly strong. (*Mark Hillier Collection*)

The last time I saw Joe was when I picked him up in March 2017 to take him out for the day. My son George adored Joe. We took him to the Tangmere Military Aviation Museum as he was still as fired up about flying and engineering as he ever had been. George led him around, holding onto Joe's finger. Sadly, only a few weeks later he passed away. (*Mark Hillier Collection*)

Joe's medal group, representing, left to right, the 1939-45 Star, France and Germany Star, Defence Medal, War Medal, General Service Medal with Malaya Bar, RAF Good Conduct and Long Service Medal, and, lastly, the *Légion d'honneur* awarded for his part in the air operations after D-Day. To the top right is his original King's Crown cap badge. (*Mark Hillier Collection*)